SIR LOIN

WASSAIL

SEYMOUR

CHRISTMAS

INVENTING

CHRISTMAS

HOW OUR HOLIDAY

CAME TO BE

JOCK ELLIOTT

HARRY N. ABRAMS, INC., PUBLISHERS

For my Elly

Thank you for the past

fifty-five years of happiness.

With all my love and a very

Merry Christmas!

Dear Santa Claus,
birdie wants some
Birdseed, and some
sugar candy, and
something for him
to peck to make his bill

sharp.

From Jock and Baby.

Dear Santa Claus
    I would like a 22 rifle
punching bag electric crain
kodak type writer water pistal.
Foot ball suit sport glass roller
skates some books ~~Black Buccaneer~~
the book of pirates, A butterflies
net a running punts and I am
8 years old a pair of ice shates
a pair of dumbbells and
the three Musketeers,
and an airplane called a
glider.
        Jock Elliott

TOM TUCKER

Dear Santa Claus, I
want a dirigible that
goes by machinery about
two feet and a half long
made by steel,
I want a belt in my
stocking and a CHRISTMas

TREE, I want ~~a pen~~   I want a tamahawk and
and ~~a motor car~~ and   a real soldier suit
some money to buya   with a sword and a
ranch. I want an ~~Indian gun.~~
~~suit~~ and a bigger
bicycle with a horn.
~~I want an airplane and~~
some neckties and a
~~biger sled~~ and ~~cowboy~~
~~boots~~ and some moccasins
and a pair of new shoes.
I want a clowns suit.

Dear Santa Clause,

    I would like a fountain pen and pencil, a big trick box, an electric steam roller, roller skates, and a christmas tree. I would also like a "woolsey football game" and a

Dear Santa Claus please put some life-savers in our stocking.

INTRODUCTION

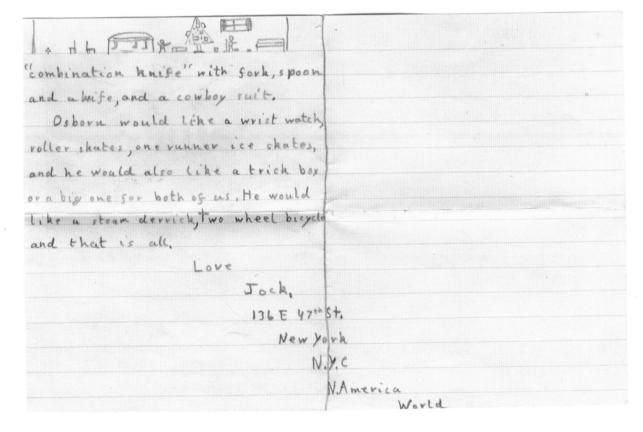

"combination knife" with fork, spoon and a knife, and a cowboy suit.

    Osborn would like a wrist watch, roller skates, one runner ice skates, and he would also like a trick box or a big one for both of us. He would like a steam derrick, two wheel bicycle and that is all.

           Love

              Jock,

              136 E 47th St.

                New York

                  N.Y.C

                  N.America

                    World

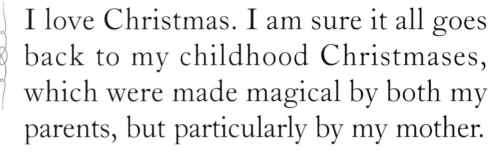

Page two: Frontispiece from The Book of Christmas, *1836, by Thomas K. Hervey.*

Pages 6-7: Letters to Santa 1926-28. Going on eight years old, my handwriting was a lot better than now, going on eighty-two.

Opposite: Christmas morning, 1937. I seem bemused by the trick golf club Santa has left me. Below: Christmas morning, 1944. I had just returned from the war in the Pacific, and my brother had just left for it. Our mother shows her presents from us.

I love Christmas. I am sure it all goes back to my childhood Christmases, which were made magical by both my parents, but particularly by my mother.

My mother, an only child, grew up in a broken family. I don't recall her ever speaking of *her* childhood Christmases—never a word about the happy bustle of the season, the secret presents, the carol singing, the bulging stocking, the glittering tree, the family get-togethers, the turkey and the plum pudding, the games. Come Christmas, she must have been a lonely little girl. Oh, how she made up for it when her own family, with two little boys, came along.

I remember the family excursions downtown to pick the perfect

tree—a ten-footer for $10; a hand-made wooden stand and delivery cost a dollar extra (it was a long time ago). I remember tucking my letter to Santa Claus inside the chimney on Christmas Eve. I recently came across a batch of the letters my baby brother Osborn and I wrote to Santa (our mother obviously had saved them all). In one, I wanted a "cowboy suit"; in another, he (age five) asked for a machine gun!

I remember the "early morning" presents Osborn and I found at the foot of our beds on Christmas morning. They were to keep us quiet until stocking-time. My brother and I still give each other early morning presents. We give them to our wives, too, never fear.

I remember the excitement of going downstairs to the tree Santa had decorated in the night . . . first the scent of balsam and then the dazzle of the lights. I remember the piles of presents, even during the Great Depression, although I guess my parents had fewer presents in those days. I remember the little white tree on the dining-room table with silver baubles and lighted candles. I remember . . . ah, well.

As I grew older, I became swept up in the festival spirit of Christmas in New York City. It still happens to me. I love the great tree at Rockefeller Center and go out of my way, again and again, to take a look. I love the parade of lighted trees down Park Avenue, with the giant lighted cross at the end, and the colored blinking lights in the windows of the less-swell neighborhoods.

I love the sidewalk whiffs of roasting chestnuts, the clanging of the Salvation Army bells, the Ho! Ho! Hos! of a hundred Santa Clauses. I love the store windows, the crowds of shoppers with their parcels, the merrymaking, three deep, in all the bars. I love the candlelit church services that herald the birth of Jesus and the peace that settles over the city late on Christmas Eve. The whole world seems to hold its breath. On Christmas morning, I love the cries of "Merry Christmas!" and the smiles. I love Christmas!

For most people Christmas comes but once a year. Not so for me. I have collected Christmas books for the past fifty years— books of stories, poems, and carols, books about the customs and traditions of Christmas, books of Yuletide illustrations, light hearted books for children and heavy books for scholars, even medieval illuminated manuscripts—all qualify.

Friends often ask me how many Christmas books I have. Of course, it is a meaningless statistic. They range from near-junk to unique rarity. For the

Below: The most endearing, enduring Christmas image from my childhood. Thank you, Jessie Willcox Smith. 1912.

Opposite: The glorious title page from The Child's Christmas *by the great English illustrator, Charles Robinson. 1906.*

The Child's Christmas

PICTURED BY CHARLES ROBINSON

WITH TEXT BY EVELYN SHARP

BLACKIE AND SON LIMITED

LONDON · GLASGOW
DUBLIN · BOMBAY

record, I own more than three thousand first editions (I have never counted them). Now it is my turn to write one.

Over time, I have learned quite a bit about Christmas. I learned how Puritans attacked Christmas in both Europe and the New World and tried to abolish it altogether. It would never be quite the same again. Later, I found that many of our age-old customs, like the giving of Christmas presents, were not so age-old after all. Did you know that when George Washington became president, there was no such thing as Christmas shopping, Christmas trees were virtually unheard of, it would be another quarter of a century before Santa Claus appeared on the scene, and the first Christmas card would have to wait for fifty years? All of these "traditions" had yet to be invented.

The concept of invented traditions is not new. But it recently occurred to me that most of our Christmas customs were invented in an amazingly short twenty-five-year period, from 1823 to 1848—a sort of "Big Bang" of our Christmas.

The exception that proves the rule is the tradition of Christmas carols. This is our only custom that does not fit my Big Bang thesis, if you will. In fact, the years 1823–1848 marked a low point for the carol tradition. However, the story of carols is interesting, and I have included a chapter on it.

This book deals mainly with the secular, festival aspects of Christmas, rather than the religious. All of the illustrations are

Opposite: Adoration of the Magi, *from a fifteenth-century Book of Hours.*

from my collection, and the sources are all to be found in my books. However, the versions of events very often differ from one another. Take the matter of the earliest Christmas trees in this country. In 1961, Miles and John Hadfield wrote in their well-researched book, *The Twelve Days of Christmas*: "Indeed, there is evidence of a Christmas tree being used by the German settlers in Pennsylvania as early as 1746." In 1995, Professor Stephen Nissenbaum wrote in his scholarly *The Battle for Christmas*: "… it seems plain that credible evidence of actual Christmas trees [in Pennsylvania] dates no earlier than the 1810s."

Differences are not surprising, since the truth is often hidden in the mists and myths of long ago. In such cases, I have blithely picked what seems to me the most likely version.

I don't want to tell you more than you want to know about how our Christmas was invented, but for those who would like to know more about this subject and the customs and traditions of Christmas in general I have included a bibliography.

I hope you enjoy the book, and I wish you many a Merry Christmas!

JOCK ELLIOTT

I

LONG AGO

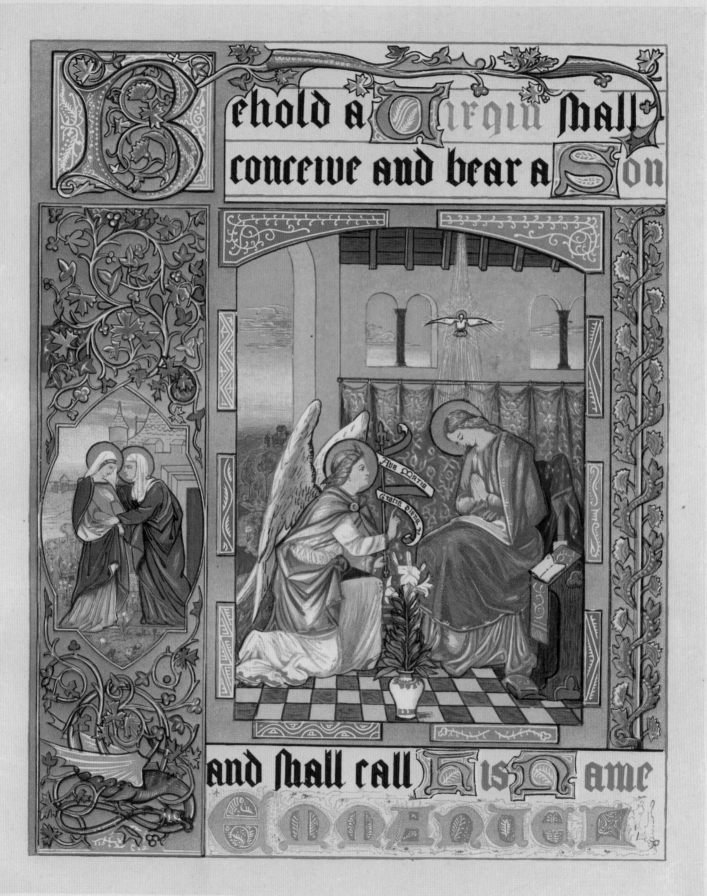

Beginning at the dawn of civilization, the peoples of the Northern Hemisphere celebrated at the time of the winter solstice. They had good reason to do so. Theirs were agrarian societies, and the annual return of the sun provided the promise that planting would soon begin again, that life would go on.

These celebrations honored the pagan gods on whom these early societies relied for their crops and general welfare. It was a time to let off steam; the work for the year was pretty much done. The harvest was in; livestock, which had fattened in the fields of summer, but could not be fed through the winter, had been slaughtered. The fresh meat had to be eaten quickly before it spoiled (or cured for later, less palatable consumption). There was plenty of other food and newly brewed drink. Heigh-ho! Feast and drink away!

The years passed, thousands of them. In the Roman world, the midwinter festival fell in two parts. First came the Saturnalia, in honor of Saturn, the god of harvest, beginning on December 17 and lasting seven days. Several days later came the Kalends of January, celebrating the New Year.

The festivities were marked by civilized goodwill as well as by barbaric hedonism. Warfare was suspended, businesses were closed, homes and places of worship were decorated with greenery and light, and gifts were given, especially to the children.

Gambling with cards and dice was allowed for the holidays. Men dressed up in animal skins or as women. Sex was rampant.

Roles were reversed; slaves were served by their masters. Both slaves and masters ate and drank themselves insensible; they would lurch to the vomitorium and stagger back for the next course. One way or another, everyone had a very good time. It was into this ancient world that the Christian faith was born two thousand years ago.

The early Christian Church struggled to become established. Its leaders understood the powerful hold the midwinter festival had on pagan worshipers. December 25 was celebrated in honor of Mithra, the sun-god. Mithraism, originally a Persian cult, had much in common with Christianity. Its beliefs included monotheism, baptism, a doctrine of an Intercessor and Redeemer, a future life, and judgment to come. However, it had one great competitive weakness. Mithra gave no place to women, whereas Christianity held that women have souls and are equal to men.

Despite this, Mithraism posed a real threat to Christianity; it is not surprising that, in the middle of the fourth century, the Church decreed that henceforth the 25th of December would be recognized as the Day of Christ's Nativity. The Church hoped to draw the pagans from worship of the sun-god to worship of the Son of God.

This ploy worked—in one way. Within a century, the pagans had finally been won over; their cults had all but disappeared. But in another way, it backfired. The pagans were willing to become Christians, but they had no intention of giving up all the hijinks of their midwinter festival. So, what came to be known as Christmas developed a split personality: religious and secular, sacred and profane.

This dual nature of Christmas observance, pious and pagan, continued through the centuries.

Opposite: A leaf from The Golden Legend *printed by William Caxton, 1483. This is the first account of the Nativity printed in English.*

Below: Illuminated manuscript from a fifteenth-century Book of Hours. Gold, frankincense, and myrrh might be thought of as the first Christmas presents.

And ladde with hym the Virgyne marie his wyf / And whan they were co
men theder / By cause the hostryes were
alle taken vp / they were constrayned
to be with oute in a comyn place where
alle peple wente / And ther was a sta
ble for an asse that he brought with hym
and for an oxe / In that nyght our bles
sid lady and moder of god was dely
uerd of our blessyd sauyour vpon the
heye that laye in the racke / At whiche
Natiuite our lord shewde many mer-
uaylles / So by cause that the worlde
was in so grete pees / the Romayns had
don made a teple / whiche was named
the temple of pees / On whiche they co-
seylled wyth Appollo / to knowe how
longe it sholde stonde and endure /
Appollo answerd to them that it shal
stode as longe / tyl a mayde had brought
forth and born a chylde / And therfore
they dyde do wryte on the portal of ye
temple / loo this is the temple of pees
that euer shal endure / For they supposed wel / that a mayde myght neuer be
re ne brynge forth a chylde / This temple / that same tyme that our lady was
delyuerd and our lord born / ouerthre-
we & fylle alle doun / Of whiche Crys-
ten men afterward made in the same
place a chirche of our lady whiche is
callyd sca maria rotunda / that is to saye
the chirche of seynt marie the Rounde /
Also the same nyght as recordeth Inno
cent the thirde whiche was pope / that
there sprange and sourded in rome the
same nyght a wel or a fountayne / and
ran largely alle that nyght & alle that
day vnto the ryuer of Rome called Ty-
bre / Also after that recordeth saynt John
Grisostome / the thre kynges were this
nyght in theyr oryson s and prayers
vpon a montayne / whan a sterre appe
red by them whiche had the forme of a
right fayr chylde / whiche had a crosse
in his forhed / whiche sayd to these thre
kynges / that they sholde goo to Jheru

thre natures assembled in one persone /
Also Octauian themperour / like as Innocent recordeth / That he was moche desy
red of his counseyll and of his people /
that he sholde doo men worshippe hym as
god / For neuer had ther be to fore
hym so grete a maistre and lord of the
worlde as he was / Thenne themperour
sente for a prophetesse named Sebyle /
for to demande of her / yf ther were ony
so grete and lyke hym in therthe / Or
yf ony sholde come after hym / Thus
atte hour of mydday she behelde the leue /
and sawe a cercle of golde aboute the
sonne / And in the myddle of the cercle
a mayde holdyng a chylde in her armes
Thenne she called theperour and shewde
it hym / whan Octauien sawe that / he
merueylled ouer moche / wherof Seby
le sayd to hym / hic puer maior te est /
ipsum adora / This Chylde is gretter
lord than thou art / worshippe hym /
Thenne wha themperour vnderstode that
this chylde was gretter lord tha he was
he wolde not be worshipped as god / but
worshipped this child that sholde be
born / wherfore the Cristen men made a
chircle of the same chambre of thempe
rour / and named it Ara celi / After
this it happed on a nyght / as a grete
maistre whiche is of grete auctorite in
scripture whiche is named bartilmew re
cordeth that the Vode of engaddi whi
che is by Jherusalem whiche berith bame
flowred this nyght and bare fruit and
gaf liquour of bame / After this cam
the angelle and apperid to the shepher-
des that kepte their sheep / and said to
theym / I anounce and shewe to you a
grete Joye / For the sauyour of the worlde
is in this nyght born / in the cyte of
Bethlee / there may ye fynde hym wrap
ped in clothes / And anon as the
Aungell had said this / a grete mul-
titude of angelis appered with hym / &
began to synge / honour glorye & helth
be to god on hye / And in therthe pees

Eus in adiutoni
um meum in
tende

Domine a
me festina
tua pata
em an
ment
uta imple fup
que tu aralti
emento
q̄ n̄ra quonda
bata uirginē.
mam sumple
aria mr
misericordie. t
ptege et hora
loria tib
natus es de vir

No one knows the time of year, much less the day, of Christ's birth. In fact, we don't even know the year Jesus was born. It must have been at least four or five years earlier than the date we customarily recognize.

In the Gospel According to Matthew, we find: "Now when Jesus was born in Bethlehem of Judea in the days of Herod the king, behold, wise men from the East came to Jerusalem . . ." The Gospel According to Luke also places the birth in the time of Herod, and we know that Herod died in 4 B.C.

Another explanation of the dating discrepancy: Our modern calendar is a modification of the Roman calendar introduced by Julius Caesar in 45 B.C. Caesar based his dating ab urbe condita (from the foundation of Rome). Well and good. In the sixth century a monk, Dionysius Exiguus, proposed that the Christian Era should date from the year of Christ's birth. Well and good again. However, the monk made a mistake in tallying up Roman history; he forgot the four-year reign of Emperor Octavian. Nobody's perfect.

One more bit of evidence: Tertullian, the great Christian lawyer of the early third century, reported that the birth of Jesus occurred seven or eight years before the supposed date. Censuses took place every fourteen years—A.D. 20, 34 and 48. Counting backward, previous censuses would have been in A.D. 6 and 8 B.C. So when Luke wrote: "In those days a decree went out from Caesar Augustus that all the world should be counted," the census in which the Holy Family was included would have been in 8 B.C. , agreeing with Tertullian's estimate.

Now you know more about the date of Christ's birth than most people, which should come in handy at dinner parties, if not in church.

Opposite: The Holy Family, *from a fifteenth-century Book of Hours.*

2 Nꝏwaog, uttiyeuwoh noh neekit Jewſe ketaſſꝏt, newutche nauómun wutanogquſſeumoh wutchepwoeiyeu, kah nuppeyaumun onk woh nꝏwowuſſumoun.

3 Herod Ketaſſꝏt nꝏtog ꝏtammehukqunuſh, kah wame Jeruſalem weeche.

4 Kah wame mounont negonne ſephauſuaéneuh, & wuſ-Scribſumouh miſſinninnúog, wunnatꝏtumauuh nahog, uttohut Chriſt woh neekit?

5 Kah wuttinóuh, ut Bethlem ut Judea, newutche yeu wuttinſukwhoſin naſhpe quoſhodtumwaen.

b Mich. 5.2. John. 7.41.

6 Kah ken *b* Bethlem ohkeit Judea, matta kuppeiſſiſſu kenugke nanánuwaenuog Judah, newutche piſh na ꝏche ſohhamun nananuwaen, yeuoh piſh nánaunau nummiſſinninnámoh Iſraeloh.

7 Neit Herod kemu wehkomont waantamwoh, pahku wunnatꝏtomau nahog, toh uttꝏche anogqs naeitauóus.

8 Kah wutannꝏnuh nahog en Bethlehem kah nꝏwau, monchek pahke natinnehuk mukkies, kah namehbeog kuttuſſunau, onk woh nuppeam, kah woh nen wonk nꝏwowuſſum.

9 Kah nꝏtauákettit Sontimoh moncheog, kah kuſſeh, noh anogqs, uttoh nauábetteúpuh wutchepwóieu, negonſhauoh noh en peyonat uttoh mukkies ápit, ne wunneepaun.

10 Nauahettit ànogſoh, mꝏcheke muſkouanatamwog miſhe wekontamóonk.

11 Kah paahettit wetuómut nameheaog peiſſeſoh weeche Maryhoh okaſoh, kah penuſhaog kah ꝏwowuſſumóuh, kah woſhwunnumóhettit wunnompakouunoúoaſh, wuttinnumáouh magꝏongaſh, gold, kah frankincenſe, kah myrre.

12 Kah God ámomont ut kaeonganit matta ukquſhkeanóut en Herodut, nag chippeog panéin, nehenwonche wutohtuóut.

13 Kah amaehettit, kuſſeh wutangelumoh Lord naehtauau Joſephoh kouénat, wuttinuh, omohkiſh, kah nemun mukkies, kah ohkahſoh, kah ſpuhhꝏaſh en Egypt, kah na apſh, nó pajeh kittinnunat, newutche Herod piſh natinnewhau peiſſeſſoh, woh wunnuſhónat

14 Kah omohkeit, nemunau peiſſeſoh, kah ohkaſoh nuhkonáeu, kah au Egypt.

15 Kah na wuttaiin nó pajeh Herod nàpuk, ne woh nnih, ne anꝏwop Lord naſhpe quoſhodtumwaen, nꝏwau, wutch *c* Egypt nꝏwehkom nunnaumon.

c Hoſea 11.1.

16 Neit Herod nag ꝏnambeûhkannaonganꝏ waantamwog, muſquantam mꝏcheke, kah anꝏteamꝏ kah paguanon wame mukkiog ut Bethlem, kah ut waéwenu, wehque neeſwe kodtumwohkogig, kah papeiſſiſſecheg, papaume ne uttꝏche pahke natꝏtomauont waantamwoh.

17 Neit n nihyeup toh anꝏwodt *d* Jeremias quoſhodtumwaen nꝏwop.

d Jere. 31.15.

18 Wudtauatonkquſſuonk ut Ramah nꝏtamun, neuánatamoonk, mauonk, kah mauémꝏonk mꝏcheke, Rachel maiémon uppeiſſéſimoh, kah matta hahkꝏwaou, newutche nag matchaog.

19 Qut Herod napuk, kuſſeh wutangelumoh Lord naeihtauau ut koueonganit Joſephuh ut Egypt.

20 Nꝏwau, omohkiſh, neemun mukkies kah ohkaſoh, kah monchiſh ohkit Iſrael, newutche nag nuppꝏk kodtinneanoncheg mukkieſoh.

21 Neit omohkeu, kah nemunau mukkoiéſoh, kah okaſoh, kah peyau ohkit Iſrael.

22 Qnt nꝏtog Archilaus piahquttum Judea, nompuppehtauau ꝏthoh Herod, wabeſu nohoonat: qut ámomont God koueonganit, quſhken en ohkeit Galile.

23 Kah paont wutapen Otanat uſſowetamun Nazareth, ne woh nnih ne anꝏwop, qnoſhodtumwaen piſh wuttiſſoweſu wun-Nazaren.

CHAP. III.

KAh yeuſh ut keſukodtaſh John *a* Baptiſt peyau kuhkꝏtomuhteau ut touohkomuk Judea.

a Mark 1.4. Luke. 3.2.

2 Kah nꝏwau, Aiuſkoianatamꝏk, newutche keſukque wutaſſꝏtamoonk paſꝏcheyeuꝏ.

3 Newutche yeuoh noh anꝏwohpoh Eſaias quoſhodtumwaen nꝏwau, *b* Wuttauatonkquſſuonk paſuk miſhontꝏadt ut tauohkomuk, nanaſhwehtamꝏk ummay Lord, ayimꝏk ummayaſh ſampoiyeuut.

b Iſáy. 40.3. Mark. 1.3.

4 Kah yeuoh John hogkꝏ weſhagkanꝏaſh kamels, kah wunnagas puttugquoppiſſu, kah ummeetſuonk locuſts kah touohkomukque hony.

5 Neit Jeruſalem kah wame Judea, kah wame penuohkomuk quinnuppu Jordan wuſſohwehtunkquoh.

6 Kah baptizuog naſhpe nagum ut Jordan ſampꝏàhettit ummatcheſeonganꝏaſh.

7 Qut nauont monaog Phariſeſog & Sadduceſog peyauoh ut ukkutſumꝏonganit, wuttinuh nahoh, Woi kenaau *c* wutontſeonganꝏ ſeſéquáog, howan kutámomukkóuóus wuſſeemoun wutch muſquantamóonk paonukqueꝏg.

c Mat. 12.34.

8 Yowutche padtauok meechummuongaſh yaneunkquokiſh aiuſkoiantamóonk.

9 Kah ahque unnantamꝏk woh kuſſinneau ut kuhhogkaóut nꝏſhun *d* Abraham nutahtauunán, newutche kuttinnonnumwꝏ, God tapenum wutchéheun yeu quſſukqunéhtu wunnaumonuh Abraham.

d John. 8.39.

10 Kah eyeu wonk togkunk padtohkuhkon wutchóhquom matugqut, yowutche *e* niſh noh paſuk matug matta adtannegenunꝏg meeꝏ

e Mat. 7.19.

Opposite: A leaf of the first account of the Nativity printed in America from the Indian Bible, translated into the Algonquian language by John Eliot, 1663.

Below: Bringing in the Yule Log.

From the Middle Ages until the Reformation, the royal courts of Europe set the Christmas pace. Long church services, with ponderous, mind-numbing sermons were offset by the most elaborate festivities; plays and masques were performed. The cost of a single masque, with its extravagant costumes, could run to thousands of pounds—all for one or two performances. The consumption of food and drink was mind-boggling. The first course of a dinner might consist of sixteen to twenty dishes washed down with gallons of wine and ale. Lords of Misrule were elected to preside over the festivities (harking back to the pagan custom of role reversal).

BRINGING IN THE YULE LOG.   [*Frontispiece.*

By the time of the Reformation, the vulgar, pagan celebrations of Christmas had so overshadowed the religious that the reformers finally put their foot down. They argued that there was no biblical or historical reason to place the birth of Jesus on December 25; if God had wanted the anniversary of the Nativity to be observed, He would have at least given a clue as to when the event took place. They argued that the excessive festivities of the holiday not only had nothing to do with true Christian tradition, they actually violated it.

In 1647, under Oliver Cromwell, an act of Parliament forbade the observance of Christmas. In 1659, under the Puritan government in Massachusetts, it became *illegal* to celebrate Christmas. The Puritans decided that since they couldn't Christianize Christmas, they would abolish it altogether. Christmas was actually stricken from the church calendar.

All of this ignited a warfare of pamphlets propounding, and attacking, the Puritans' position. For a few years, Christmas went underground.

It turned out that the festival spirit could not be killed in the seventeenth century any more than in the fourth. Charles II revived the holiday in England after the Restoration, and the

1659 law in the colonies was revoked in 1681. Even so, it took a while for Christmas to recover from the cold water poured upon it by the Puritans. In the eighteenth century, Christmas slowly recovered, although in different ways for different segments of society. For some, Christmas still had no significance whatsoever. Among the young there was strong reaction to earlier Puritan restrictions. Drinking and sex were all the rage. Premarital pregnancies ballooned; a bulge of births in September and October was the tip-off to hanky panky at Christmastime.

For many of the young and the lower classes, Christmas became a time of carnival, carnival gone bad. By the mid-1700s, music composed for Christmas had become popular. Nothing insidious about that except for the use to which it was often put: roughhouse wassailing that could border on violence. Wassailers would force their way into homes and demand rewards for their obnoxious behavior.

Above left: Bringing in the Boar's Head.

Above right: Pamphlet in defense of the celebration of Christmas, 1647.

Opposite: One of the earliest Christmas books for children, c. 1788, written more for their instruction than amusement (the little poem gives the game away!).

See here the Youth by *Wisdom*'s precepts led,
The peaceful Paths of Life securely tread;
The dang'rous Lures of *Folly* safely shun,
And *Virtue*'s pleasant course serenely run,

CHRISTMAS TALES

FOR THE

AMUSEMENT and INSTRUCTION

OF

Young LADIES and GENTLEMEN

IN

WINTER EVENINGS.

By SOLOMON SOBERSIDES.

The chearful Sage, when solemn Dictates fail,
Conceals the moral Counsel in a — Tale.

LONDON:

Printed by *J. Marshall* and Co. No. 4, in *Aldermary Church Yard*, who have ordered all the *Booksellers*, both in *Town* and *Country*, to make a Present of it to Good Girls and Boys, they paying Six-pence only to defray the Expences of Binding.

TUESDAY,　　　　　THE　　　　　DECEMBER 25, 1781.

Pennsylvania Packet

OR, THE
GENERAL ADVERTISER.

VOL. XI.]　PUBLISHED EVERY TUESDAY, THURSDAY AND SATURDAY.—Price SIX-PENCE.　[NUMB 824.

The higheſt Price is given for clean Linen and Cotton RAGS, by the Printer of this Paper.

A Further SALE of the

Public Lots of this City,

For the redemption of the Bills of Credit of this ſtate, dated April the 29th, 1780, will be held at the Coffee-houſe, on THURSDAY, the 3d of January next, at TEN o'clock in the forenoon. A Plan of the Lots may be ſeen at the Coffee-houſe, and at the Surveyor General's Office. The conditions the ſame as the laſt ſales.

In the Court of Admiralty of Pennſylvania.

Nicholas Martin qui tam, &c. 　 Supplemental Bill
vs. 　 by Benjamin Allen
The Schooner Dolly and Cargo. 　 and others part of the crew belonging to the privateer Brigantine Neſbit.

December 13th, 1781. Rule taken by conſent in this Cauſe—

THAT if any perſon named in the libel or ſupplemental bill in this cauſe will on or before the firſt day of January next produce to his honour the Judge any further evidence to prove that any individual of the crew belonging to the privateer brig Neſbit did deſert from the ſaid brig or if any perſon belonging to the ſaid crew againſt whom deſertion is alledged will on or before the ſaid day offer to his Honour proof that he did not deſert from the ſaid brig ſuch proof will be received and conſidered—otherwiſe a decree will paſs upon the evidence now before the court.
Publiſhed by order of the Judge,
JAMES READ, Regiſter.

Will be wanted in eight or ten Days from this date, Twenty good TEAMS, to go to Carolina; they will be engaged by the Trip or Mile; to find their own Proviſions and Forage. Enquire of SAMUEL MILES, D. Q. M.
Philadelphia, December 17, 1781.

Charles Pettit,

AT the houſe of the late William Allen, eſquire, in Water-ſtreet, a few doors ſouthward of Market-ſtreet, hath for SALE, by the Bale or Piece, for Caſh, Bills of Exchange, or Bank Notes,

A FEW bales of low priced Blankets,
Two pieces of light Sail Duck,
Low priced blue and brown Cloths,
Coatings and Swanſkins,
A ſmall Aſſortment of Linens, from fine ſhirting linen to dowlaſs,
A few pieces of Cambrick,
Some Ribbons, Silk Laces, &c.

At the ſame Place may alſo be had,

A few pair of Cannon, 9 and 6 pounders,
Cannon Shot from 6 to 24 pounders,
Grape Shot,
Rolled Iron ſuitable for cabooſes,

Which he will ſell to the firſt appliers, on moderate terms, in order to cloſe the ſales.

Adam Zantzinger,

AT his STORE in Market-ſtreet, between Third and Fourth-ſtreets, hath for Sale, by the Invoice or ſmaller Quantity, on reaſonable Terms,

A VERY large Aſſortment of ſuperfine and common Broadcloths, coarſe Coatings, Shalloons and Trimings, Flanells, Serges, ſilk and worſted Hoſe, Chintzes and Calicoes, Brittannias and other Linens, ſewing Silk and Thread, ſilk Ribbons and Umbrellos; and many other Articles too tedious to enumerate.

N. B. Likewiſe a Pair of ſtout Carriage HORSES, in good order, and a PHÆTON, with Harneſs, which will be ſold reaſonable, or exchanged for beſt Virginia Tobacco.

Juſt Imported, in the Ship Anne, from France, and to be SOLD, By

Mifflin and Butler,

AT their Store on South-ſtreet Wharf, A Variety of DRY GOODS ſuitable to the Seaſon: Among which are the following Articles,

FINE and coarſe Blankets,
Blue Halfthicks,
Second Cloths;
White Flanells and Swanſkins;
Camblets,
Striped and checked Cottons,
Naps,
Fine and coarſe Flanders Sheeting,
White and brown Britagns, Picardy, Nonbuttu, and Royal Laval Linens,
Sail Canvas, No, 1, 2, 3, and 4,
A 12 and a half inch Cable, and 4-inch Shroud Haulter, both excellent, and a Quantity of ſheet Lead.

IMPORTED in the ſhip Ann, Captain Joſiah, from l'Orient, and to be Sold by

Andrew Tybout,

In Cheſnut-ſtreet, viz.

WHITE Coatings, Swanſkins, Blankets, Chintzes and Calicoes, wide and narrow Brittannias, Nonbattu and Laval Linens, Sail Twine, wide and narrow Velvet Binding, Hat Linings, Looping, Bowſtrings, Oil of Vitreol, Verdigreaſe, &c. &c.
Said TYBOUT alſo has for Sale, a Quantity of Beaver and Jeſuits Bark.

Michael Morgan Obrien,

AT his Store on the weſt ſide of Front-ſtreet, five doors below Cheſnut-ſtreet, will diſpoſe of the following GOODS for Caſh, Bills of Exchange, or the Produce of the Country:

Nonbattu and Laval Linens,

A great Variety of Sheeting,
Fine Brittannias,
Printed Cottons and Chintzes, dark ground,
Flanders Bedticks, compleat,
Firſt and ſecond Broadcloths,
Superfine white Flannel,
Coatings,
Poland Starch,
Jamaica and cane juice Spirit,
Rum and Muſcovado Sugar in barrels.

JONAS PHILLIPS,

AT his STORE, the South ſide of Market ſtreet, between Front and Second-ſtreets, Philadelphia;

A LARGE Aſſortment of DRY GOODS, of various KINDS, which he will diſpoſe of by whole-ſale at a very reaſonable price, either for gold or ſilver, Pennſylvania ſtate money, tobacco or flour, &c.

He takes the liberty to acquaint his friends and cuſtomers, that he has opened his ſtore for the reception or all kind of merchandize on commiſſion; where conſtant attendance will be given, and the utmoſt care and diligence, will be uſed in diſpoſing of the goods ſoon, and to the beſt advantage, and the money paid on demand. Captains of veſſels, with their ſupercargoes, who daily arrive in this city, being ſtrangers and not knowing where to diſpoſe of their goods, if they will pleaſe to call at the commiſſion ſtore, they will always find ſtorage and a ready ſale for their goods—for which they may receive gold or ſilver, ſtate money, bills of exchange, Virginia and Maryland tobacco, flour, and other country produce, &c.　Nov. 26, 1781.

STAYED or ſtolen, out of Greenwich meadows, near the Point houſe, the latter end of laſt month, Two Black HORSES; one a likely horſe, about 15 hands high, with a ſtar and ſome of his feet white, with a long tail, 4 or 5 years old, natural trotter; the other about 14 hands and a half high, crooked hind legs, paces moſtly, about 5 or 6 years old: Alſo, an old Black COW, with ſome white on her belly, branded on the horns J. Penroſe. The ſubſcriber has a ſtray Bay HORSE, about 14 hands high; he came into the above meadows with a rope about his neck. The owner is deſired to come, pay charges, and take him away. Four Dollars will be given for each Horſe, Eight if ſtolen, and Two Dollars for the Cow.
JONATHAN PENROSE.
Philadelphia, Dec. 15.

A Negro Woman to be Sold.

SHE is a good houſe and chamber ſervant, can waſh, iron, milk, and ſew plain work, is very handy and likely, and is free from the faults of ſtealing and drunkenneſs.

Twenty Pounds Specie Reward.

WAS broke open, laſt night, the houſe of Levi Hollingſworth, and the following ARTICLES ſtolen;
6 ſilver Table ſpoons, marked H P.
5 ditto Tea-ſpoons,　　ditto.
　　　　　　　　　　　　H
4 ditto, ditto,　　　L. H.
1 ditto Cream-pot,　C A H in a cypher.
1 ditto Sugar-Tongs,　H P.
2 pound Canniſter Tea.
2 half-gallon Bowls of enamelled China.
1 quart Decanter of Wine.
1 Razor in a caſe, Razors marked A, B, C, and Caſe L. H.
1 large damaſk Tablecloth, L. H.
1 ſmall ditto,　ditto,　ditto.
　　　APPREHENDED.
1 drab Great-Coat, with cloth Cape, half worn, letter V. in the cape.
2 mens Beaver Hats, one cocked the other round, bound with edging.
1 pair mens Boots.
3 pair and one odd mens worſted Stockings new, and run in the heels.
11 ditto, old.
4 ditto, yarn, ribbed, 3 pair of which was white, the the other mixed blue.
2 ditto womens worſted ditto.

Silverſmiths and others are requeſted to ſtop ſaid Goods if offered for ſale, for which they ſhall be rewarded, and if the Robbers ſhall be apprehended and brought to juſtice, the above Reward and all reaſonable Charges, paid by　LEVI HOLLINGSWORTH.
Philadelphia, December 21, 1781.

To the TRADING PEOPLE of AMERICA.

M. M. Coulougnac, and Co.

MERCHANTS in Lyon, a City in France,

Will have opened and ready furniſhed with all kind of dry goods, the firſt of January, 1782, a ſtore-houſe as well in Nantes as in L'Orient, in which any one may have a general aſſortment of Cloths, Coatings, Silks, Linens, &c. &c. &c. proceeding from their own manufactures in Sedan, Louviers, Elbœuf, Lodeve, Carcaſſonne, Laval, Calma, Caſtres, French Flander, Lyon, Paris, &c. &c. &c.

M. M. Coulougnac and company, will treat of thoſe goods for money, or ſuitable bills of Exchange on every place in Europe, or in Tobacco, Indigo, Furs, ſkins, or any other production, either of North America, or Weſt India Iſlands, at the rate then current in thoſe two cities.

By the means of theſe propoſed exchanges, the merchants who will for the future ſend cargoes there may ſpare the commiſſion, and ſtorage expences, by applying to the aforeſaid gentlemen, as ſoon as their ſhips are arrived there; and by finding in M. M. Coulougnac and company's Store, all the goods their captains or agents may poſſibly deſire; their voyages will for the time to come be much ſhorter than formerly. Therefore ſaid gentlemen will likewiſe accept of the direction either of the ſhips and cargoes, or of part of them only, that one will chuſe to truſt their care in Nantes or L'Orient.

Joſeph Mercier, their agent in Philadelphia at Peter Le Maigre and company's ſtore, in Water-ſtreet, between Market and Arch-ſtreets, will take upon himſelf to receive and cauſe any one's orders and commiſſions to be carefully and in the beſt manner executed in France.

The chiefs of the French nation in all continental ſea-ports will make clear all that one could wiſh to know on the good name and ſolidity of M. M. Coulougnac and company.

To the Contractor for ſupplying the Army with Rations for the Poſt of Philadelphia, during the Year 1782.

AS the article of Beef is a material part of the Ration above, I have thought proper to make you the Propoſal of furniſhing that Article, which I will iſſue at my ſlaughter-houſe, at 45s. per hundred weight, to be paid monthly.

PETER SUMMERS.

Philadelphia, Dec. 17, 1781.

Opposite: An issue of the first American daily newspaper dated December 25, 1781, yet the word "Christmas" never once appears. How times have changed!

For the more well-to-do, feasting with friends was resumed. Even the clergy began to change their mind. It was all right to celebrate the birth of the Savior after all. Churches began to open their doors on Christmas Day.

As late as the end of the eighteenth century, there was precious little resembling the Christmas we know today—no family togetherness, no Christmas trees, no Christmas cards, no Christmas shopping, not much in the way of Christmas presents (even for children), and of course, no Santa Claus. All that, however, was soon to change. Oddly enough, the change was to be a reaction to the kind of excessive behavior that had typified the mid-winter festival since pagan times.

2

HOW OUR SANTA CLAUS
WAS INVENTED

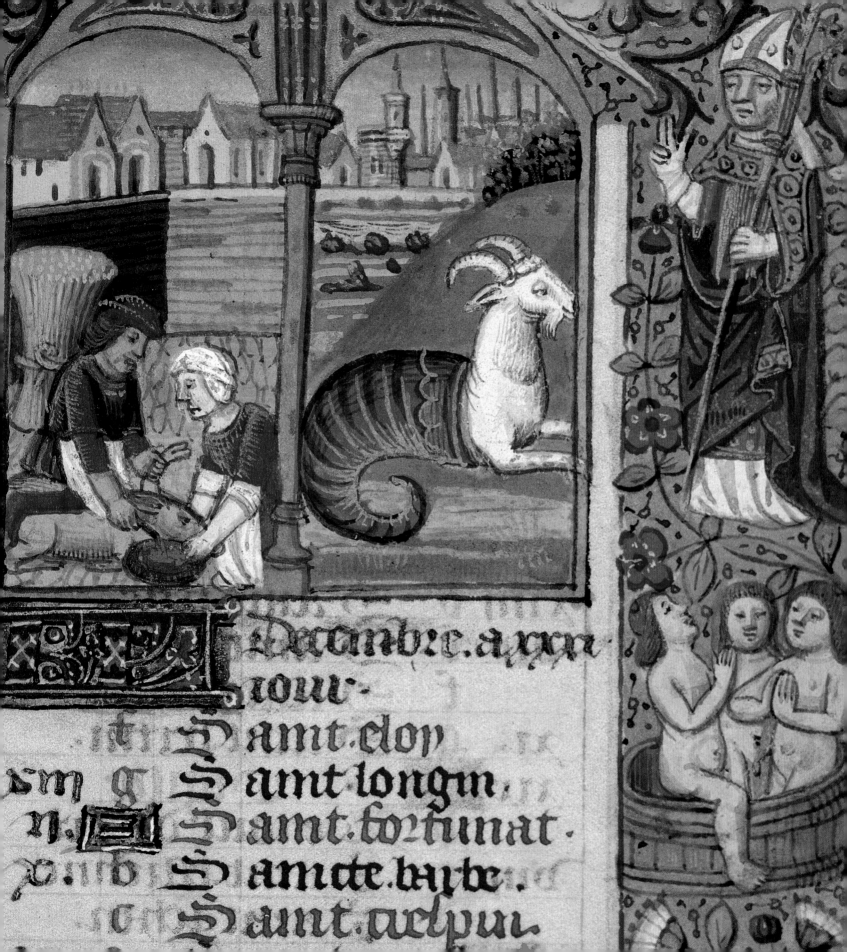

Decembre. xxxi.
tour.
Samt. eloy
Samt. longm.
Samt. fortinat.
Samte. barbe.
Samt. aelpm.

At the turn of the nineteenth century, the social order of the United States of America was in upheaval. As cities grew, so did unemployment and racial strife, and the gap between rich and poor broadened. There were widespread violent demonstrations, especially during the Christmas season, and many workers, if not laid off during the holidays, were forced to work on Christmas Day.

Previous pages: "Merry Christmas to all . . . " from A Visit from St. Nicholas, *illustrated by F. O. C. Darley, 1862.*

Opposite (detail) and below: St. Nicholas on the right with the three boys he miraculously saved. From a fifteenth-century Book of Hours.

The result was the most unruly Yuletide behavior yet. Gangs of angry, drunken hoodlums marauded the streets at Christmas and New Year's, threatening the peace and the very lives of respectable folk. Something had to change; the stage was set for a new kind of Christmas. The leading men in beginning to bring about that change were Washington Irving, John Pintard, and Clement Clarke Moore, New Yorkers all. They introduced St. Nicholas to America and invented his famous descendant, our Santa Claus.

St. Nicholas was a real man. He was born about A.D. 280 in the little city of Patara, in what is now Turkey. Nicolaos (as he was christened) was the son of relatively well-to-do Greek-speaking followers of Christ.

Nicolaos had a religious upbringing and, even before he became a priest, demonstrated the unusual caring for others that was to typify his life. A famous story has come down to us: A widowed nobleman had fallen on hard times. Penniless, he could not

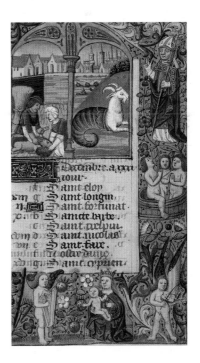

Opposite: The first illustration, in a book, of the St. Nicholas poem, 1840.

Below: The first image of St. Nicholas going down a chimney. The New-York Mirror, *January 2, 1841.*

take care of his three teenage daughters. Desperate, he considered selling the eldest into prostitution. In the middle of the night, Nicolaos threw a bag of gold through the father's window; this provided a dowry for the girl, and she was saved.

Later, again under cover of darkness, Nicolaos did this twice more, for the other two girls. The third time, the father caught him in the act. Embarrassed, and to escape the resulting notoriety, Nicolaos left home to join a religious group. Those three bags of gold live on today as the three gold balls outside of pawn-shops, symbols of something of value redeemed.

Early in his priesthood, Nicolaos became famous for performing miracles. Three had to do with saving sailors and fishermen in storms at sea. Not surprisingly, he soon became a bishop (of Myra) and was listed, years later, as one of the bishops attending the First Council of Nicaea, in A.D. 325.

One of Nicolaos' best-known miracles concerned three young

A VISIT FROM ST. NICHOLAS.

students who stopped at an inn for the night. While they were asleep, the innkeeper robbed and killed them. He cut up the bodies, salted the flesh, and put it in pickle barrels, presumably to be eaten by his other guests. Later, the bishop arrived and sensed what had happened. He miraculously brought the students back to life.

Whatever one may think of the stories and the miracles, it is obvious that Nicolaos was a remarkably good man and much beloved.

When Nicolaos died, the people (but not the Church) dubbed him Saint Nicholas. Through the centuries, the cult of St. Nicholas spread from country to country, and more and more miracles were attributed to the intercession of the good saint. In western Europe, he became the patron saint of childhood. Parents prayed to him when a child was sick or missing, with a high rate of success, according to the chronicles of the time.

Nicholas became the most popular of all saints; for a while, more churches were dedicated in his name than in the names of any of the apostles. He came to be ranked third, behind only Jesus and Mary, as a figure to be worshiped and adored.

During the Protestant Reformation, the reformers had no truck with all of this. They tried to eliminate the veneration of saints, but in Holland and Germany St. Nicholas survived—as a folklore image rather than as an ecclesiastical figure. In Holland, he was known as Sinter Claas and people celebrated December 6, his name day, when he brought children presents.

It is generally thought that when the Dutch settled New Amsterdam, they brought their beloved St. Nicholas customs with them; however, there is no evidence of St. Nicholas festivities in this country in the seventeenth and eighteenth centuries. Most Dutch settlers belonged to the Dutch Reformed Church, which shared the Puritans' antipathy to Christmas and to all

Below: The first use of the title by which we know the poem today. Among the "Other Christmas Poems" is "The Night After Christmas," one of the first takeoffs. c.1858.

Opposite: From 1850 to 1852, the "Swedish Nightingale" toured the United States under the management of P. T. Barnum. This great showman enlisted the services of Santa Claus to launch the tour.

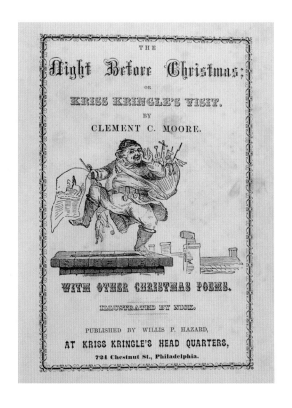

SANTA CLAUS AND JENNY LIND.

I'm a jolly old man—I ride in the wind ;
The lady behind me is Miss Jenny Lind ;
The horse that we ride is a broomstick, you see—
Oh ! this is the horse for Miss Jenny and me.

The WONDERS of SANTA-CLAUS

CHAPTER I.

CONCERNING SANTA-CLAUS,—HIS ASTONISHING CASTLE,—HIS BEAUTIFUL GIFTS FOR ALL GOOD CHILDREN,—AND HIS REAL NAME.

BEYOND the ocean many a mile,
  And many a year ago,
There lived a wonderful queer old man
  In a wonderful house of snow;
And every little boy and girl,
  As Christmas Eves arrive,
No doubt will be very glad to hear,
  The old man is still alive.

In his house upon the top of a hill,
  And almost out of sight,
He keeps a great many elves at work,
  All working with all their might,
To make a million of pretty things,
  Cakes, sugar-plums, and toys,
To fill the stockings, hung up you know
  By the little girls and boys.

It would be a capital treat be sure,
  A glimpse of his wondrous shop;
But the queer old man when a stranger comes,
  Orders every elf to stop;
And the house, and work, and workmen all
  Instantly take a twist,
And just you may think you are there,
  They are off in a frosty mist.

But upon a time a cunning boy
  Saw this sign upon the gate,
Nobody can ever enter here
  Who lies a-bed too late:
Let all who expect a good stocking full,
  Not spend too much time in play;
Keep book and work all the while in mind,
  And be up by the peep of day.

A holiday morning would scarce suffice
  To tell what was making there;
Wagons and dolls, whistles and birds,
  And elephants most rare:
Wild monkeys drest like little men,
  And dogs that could almost bark,
Watches, that, if they only had wheels,
  Might beat the old clock in the Park.

Whole armies of little soldier folk,
  All marching in grand review,
And turning up their eyes at the girls,
  As the City soldiers do.
Engines, fast hurrying to a fire,
  And many a little fool
A-trudging after them through the streets,
  Instead of going to school.

Tin fiddles, and trumpets made of wood,
  That will play as good a tune
As a Scotch bag-piper could perform
  From Christmas-day till June.
Horses, with riders upon their backs,
  Coaches, and carts, and gigs,
Each trying its best to win the race,
  Like the Democrats and Whigs.

Some little fellows turning a crank,
  And others beating a drum:
Little pianos, so exact
  You could almost hear them thrum,
Tea-sets and tables quite complete,
  With ladies sitting around,
Chatting as older ladies do,
  But a little more profound.

Steamboats made to sail in a tub,
  And fishing-smacks ahoy,
And boats and skiffs with oars and sails,
  A fleet for a sailor boy.
Ships of the line, equipt for sea,
  With officers and crew,
Each with a red cap on his head,
  And a jacket painted blue.

Bold pewter men with pistols armed,
  Like duelists so smart,
Each very wickedly taking aim
  At his little comrade's heart!
And nimble Jacks with supple joints,
  That when you pull a string,
Will give you an easy lesson how
  To dance the Pigeon Wing.

Ugly old women in a box,
  As some younger ones ought to be,
Which, when the cover is lifted off,
  Fly out most spitefully.
Ripe wooden pears like real fruit,
  Somehow made to unscrew;
Kittens with mice sewed to their mouths,
  And tabby cats crying mew.

Gay humming-tops that spin about,
  And make a senseless sound,
Like windy representatives
  In Congress often found.
Fine marbles, and rich China-men,
  That you can play from taw,
As lawyers play rich clients down
  The ring-pits of the law.

Bright caskets filled with jewelry,
  Chains, bracelets, pins, and pearls,
All glittering with tinsel, like
  Some fashionable girls.
Delightful little picture books,
  And tales of Mother Goose,
More witty than most novels are,
  And twenty times their use.

But it were an endless task to tell,
  The length that the list extends,
Of the curious gifts the queer old man
  Prepares for his Christmas friends.
Belike you are guessing who he is,
  And the country whence he came.
Why, he was born in Germany,
  And St. Nicholas is his name.

holiday celebrations that had nothing to do with Christian tradition.

It stands to reason that some of the settlers must have brought along their Sinter Claas. But whatever St. Nicholas customs may have been imported, they seem to have died out as the English took over New Amsterdam and renamed it New-York, and as the Dutch became a relatively smaller segment of New-York's growing population. There is no evidence that the cult of St. Nicholas existed in New York after the British occupied the city in 1660.

Now to the American inventors of Santa Claus. In 1809, Washington Irving wrote *Diedrich Knickerbocker's History of New York*. This was a tongue-in-cheek satire of contemporary life, in which the figure of St. Nicholas played a prominent part as the patron saint of the city. Of course, Irving knew of the Dutch veneration of St. Nicholas, but these new wrinkles were all of his own invention.

In a new edition of the *History of New York* (1821), Irving added some new inventions about St. Nicholas. He referred to his "riding over the tops of trees, in that self same waggon wherein he brings his yearly presents to children . . . the smoke from his pipe spread like a cloud overhead . . . when he had smoked his pipe, he twisted it in his hatband, and laying his finger beside his nose, gave a very significant look; then mounting his waggon, he returned over the tree tops and disappeared." This was written one year before Clement Clarke Moore wrote, "Twas the night before Christmas." We will come to Moore in a moment. In the meantime, a word about John Pintard.

John Pintard, a prosperous merchant and a leading citizen of New York, was also an antiquarian obsessed with the past. (He

MERRY CHRISTMAS TO ALL

founded the New-York Historical Society and helped establish Columbus Day, Washington's Birthday, and the Fourth of July as public holidays.) On December 6, 1810, St. Nicholas's nameday and exactly one year after the publication of Irving's *History*, Pintard held a banquet in honor of St. Nicholas. He commissioned a special poster of "Sancte Claus" for the occasion.

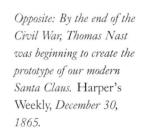

Pintard was deeply concerned about the plight of the poor and the resulting unrest and violence during the holiday season. He had an idea that a resurrection of old-time customs when rich and poor celebrated together in harmony might be the answer. The problem was that there was no tradition of celebrating December 6 in this country, and the old-time "customs" had never existed. Pintard had simply invented them for his own purposes, as had Washington Irving.

Although nothing came of his big idea, Pintard's efforts pointed up the need for change. It remained for the magic of a children's poem to begin to bring about that change. The poem, of course, was "A Visit

Opposite: By the end of the Civil War, Thomas Nast was beginning to create the prototype of our modern Santa Claus. Harper's Weekly, *December 30, 1865.*

Above: For many years, Nast contributed drawings of Santa Claus annually to Harper's Weekly. *This is one of the best known.*

Above: "Down the chimney
St. Nicholas came with a bound . . . "

Opposite: "He spoke not a word, but
went straight to his work . . . "
Both illustrations by Thomas Nast.

Left: "Merry Christmas to all, and to all a good night!" Thomas Nast.

It is surprising that Santa Claus is always associated with "The Night Before Christmas," yet Santa Claus is never mentioned in the poem! In captions to his pictures, Thomas Nast always referred to Santa Claus and never to St. Nick, thereby further entrenching Santa in our culture.

from St. Nicholas," which we know today as "The Night Before Christmas." In Clement Clarke Moore the poem had an unlikely author.

Dr. Moore was a learned man, a teacher, a scholar of Hebrew, and a serious poet (albeit a rather dreary one). He lived on a ninety-four-acre farm called Chelsea. The farm stretched from Nineteenth to Twenty-fourth Street and from Eighth to Tenth Avenue. (Today, this section of Manhattan is still called Chelsea.)

According to tradition, on the day before Christmas in 1822, Moore was driven in a sleigh down to the city (which was still confined to lower Manhattan) to buy a big Christmas turkey. On the way, he composed in his head his famous poem, which he wrote down on return. On Christmas Day, he gathered his family around him and read for the first time, "'Twas the night before Christmas . . ." Later, a family friend read the poem and was so enchanted by it that she made a copy and sent it to the *Troy Sentinel*, a newspaper in upstate New York, which published it for the first time on December 23, 1823. In 1824, it was reprinted in two almanacs, and from then on it appeared with increasing frequency until, by 1840, there could hardly have been a family in the country that was not familiar with the visit of St. Nicholas.

Tradition also has it that Moore was embarrassed by the publication. He considered the "Visit" a bit of trivial doggerel written for children, unworthy of the scholar that he was. He did not publish it under his own name for more than twenty years, until his book of poems came out in 1844.

Recently, Moore's authorship of the "Visit" has been challenged by a Vassar professor, Don Foster, whose literary detective work unmasked Joe Klein as the anonymous author of the 1996 best-selling novel, *Primary Colors*. Applying the same technique of stylistic analysis, Foster concluded that the true author of the "Visit" was Henry Livingston, Jr., a judge and amateur versifier of Poughkeepsie, New York. Livingston's descendants have been making this claim, off and on, for the past 150 years.

By all accounts, Livingston was a jolly fellow given to writing light-hearted poetry that often verged on doggerel. Moore was a somber academic, not much fun to be with. His poetry was solemn, moralistic stuff. Livingston's poems were written frequently, perhaps usually, in anapestic meter (the meter of the "Visit"). Only one of Moore's poems was written in this meter, "The Pig and the Rooster," and even it makes a moral point.

However, there are dating discrepancies in the case put forward by the Livingstons that weaken their argument. Also, it seems odd that Moore would risk jeopardizing his distinguished reputation by falsely claiming authorship of a children's poem. Although there is at least a chance that Livingston was the author, I believe that Moore wrote "A Visit from St. Nicholas"; I stand by the tradition.

Where did the ideas for the poem come from? Since Dr. Moore was a religious man, he of course knew of the legend of St. Nicholas, of the miracles attributed to him, and that he had become the patron Saint of children, sailors, and maidens. Since he was a man of learning, Moore's ideas may have come from ancient mythology. According to a German myth, on the night of the winter solstice, the great god Wotan rode through the skies on a white stallion, showering rewards on the good folk and punishment on the bad. Also in Germany, a friendly fertility sprite named Freya livened things up at Christmastime, entering people's homes on the smoke from the hearth's fire. In the Scandinavian countries, the god Thor was supposed to travel the night skies in a chariot drawn by two large goats named Cracker and Gnasher.

Moore also had sources much closer to home. As we have seen, one of these was Irving's *History of New York*, and another Pintard's 1810 poster showing St. Nicholas bringing gifts to children. Another inspiration for the poem was even more immediate: In 1821, a little children's book was published in New York. It showed Santa Claus with a reindeer. Underneath were these lines:

Above: W. W. Denslow, illustrator of The Wizard of Oz, *drew his own Santa Claus. Note the Tin Woodman! 1902.*

Opposite: Arthur Rackham was one of the most popular illustrators of the early twentieth century.

Old Santeclaus with much delight
His reindeer drives the frosty night
O'er chimney tops and tracks of snow
To bring his yearly gifts to you.

This was the first written reference to reindeer. The publisher of the little book was William B. Gilley, a friend and neighbor of

THE NIGHT BEFORE
CHRISTMAS

THE EVERETT SHINN
Illustrated Edition

CLEMENT CLARKE MOORE

EVERETT SHINN 1942

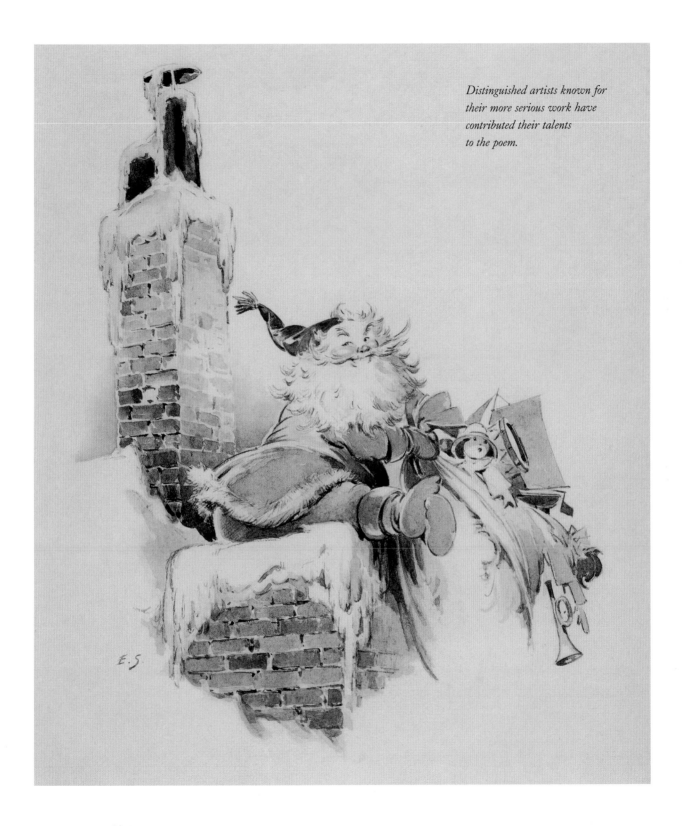

*Distinguished artists known for
their more serious work have
contributed their talents
to the poem.*

Dr. Moore. It seems likely that this is where the idea of actually writing the poem came from.

Although Moore had many sources, he did plenty of inventing himself. He was the first to draw a word picture of St. Nicholas: "Chubby and plump, a right jolly old elf ✚His eyes how they twinkled, his dimples how merry, His cheeks were like roses, his nose like a cherry ✚He had a broad face, and a little round belly that . . . " well, you get the picture. Moore also invented the eight tiny reindeer and fixed once and for all the date and the time of St. Nick's visit—not Saint Nicholas Day or Eve, not New Year's Day or Eve, not Christmas Day, but "'twas the night before Christmas."

Now I ask you to think of the true significance of this poem. I do not think it is much of an exaggeration to say that it liberated childhood. In the eighteenth century, children were not thought of as children but as miniature adults. Reading material, other than schoolbooks, consisted almost entirely of instructional matter written not for their entertainment, but for their improvement. "A Visit from St. Nicholas" was the first work of any consequence written purely for the enjoyment of children. Suddenly, Christmas was for children.

Also, throughout the eighteenth century, Christmas festivities, such as there were, were primarily public affairs, having little to do with family. The celebrations took place outside the home, often threatening the peace and security of respectable households. This poem takes place in the home, a scene of domestic tranquility. The "clatter" on the lawn outside is not caused by drunken wassailers but by an elf and his eight tiny reindeer. Now there is "nothing to dread." Christmas had become a family affair.

A new tradition had been born that was invented by Washington Irving, John Pintard, and Clement Clarke Moore.

Below and following pages: A blizzard of Santa Claus books hit the market at the end of the nineteenth century.

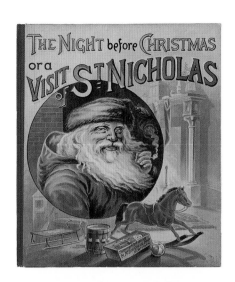

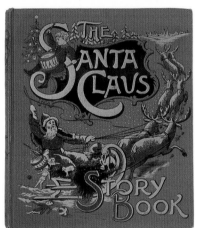

Most inventions are improved over time. This turned out to be so with "The Night Before Christmas." One illustrator after another tried his hand at portraying Santa Claus. At first, the depictions added little or nothing to the appeal of the poem. Santa was shown as a gaunt, somber old man, in the pictorial tradition of the venerable saint. He was also shown as a rather unattractive little gnome or as a clownish figure. (Looking at such an illustration, one might well wonder if the artist had even read the poem!)

By the time of the Civil War, along came Thomas Nast, a young German immigrant who was to earn fame as a political cartoonist, creating the Tammany Tiger, the Republican Elephant, and the Democratic Donkey. He also invented the visual prototype of the Santa Claus we know today, and much of the Santa Claus lore. For example, he invented the location of Santa's workshop at the North Pole, as well as Santa's custom of keeping books on good little girls and boys.

At the age of twenty-two, Nast began covering the Union side of the Civil War for *Harper's Weekly*. His first published drawing of Santa Claus appeared in the January 3, 1863 issue of that magazine. Santa, facing Union troops, is seated beneath the Stars and Stripes and is wearing a star-spangled shirt and striped pants. He bears no relationship whatsoever to our Santa Claus but is a combination of Moore's St. Nicholas and Germany's gnomelike Pelz-Nicol ("fur-Nicholas"), as Nast remembered him from his recent childhood. By the end of the Civil War, Nast was beginning to hit his Santa-stride, portraying him as an ever jollier St. Nick. Nast went on to provide *Harper's* with a Christmas illustration, usually of Santa, each year until 1886.

Since Nast, the greatest illustrators, including W. W. Denslow, Jessie Willcox Smith, Arthur Rackham, and Everett Shinn, have contributed their own distinctive charms to "The Night Before Christmas." But no one outside of Moore himself (or was it Livingston?) was as responsible for the invention of Santa Claus as Thomas Nast.

3

GIFT BOOKS AND
THE BEGINNING OF
CHRISTMAS SHOPPING

ATLANTIC SOUVENIR

1828.

CAREY LEA & CAREY,

PHILADA.

Even if you are a bibliophile, there is a good chance that you have never heard of the "gift book" fad that swept England and the United States in the second quarter of the nineteenth century. It played an important role in the development of the Christmas we know today.

When you go Christmas shopping, you can thank (or curse, as the case may be) the fad of gift books for starting it all. Human beings have always given each other presents, as expressions of goodwill, friendship, and love; the Romans exchanged gifts during their midwinter festival, and the gifts to the Baby Jesus of gold, frankincense, and myrrh might be thought of as the first Christmas presents.

The giving of Christmas presents was never the formalized tradition it is today. In colonial America, a holiday gift might consist of a side of bacon, or some molasses for pie-making. A store-bought gift was a rarity. Christmas shopping was unheard of. Then came the gift books.

Gift books were "literary annuals"—compilations of stories, poems and essays, ranging from potboilers to great literature—designed to be given to ladies, primarily at Christmastime, by their admirers as "an object of kindness and esteem." Gift books were also printed for juveniles. Various series of the books were printed under such names as gifts, tokens, forget-me-nots, keepsakes, and offerings.

Based on German and French models, the first English gift book was *Forget Me Not: A Christmas and New Year's Present for 1823*. This was so successful that it was immediately followed by a second *Forget Me Not*, and by *Friendship's Offering: A Christmas or New Year's Gift for 1824*. These proved so popular that nine gift books were printed in England the following year.

American publishers were slow to catch on, but in December, 1825, *The Atlantic Souvenir, 1826* was published as a gift for Christmas and the New Year. By 1831 the fad had become a craze: sixty-nine gift books were published, fifty-five in England and fourteen in the United States! By the 1840s, American gift books were outnumbering British, with more than sixty being printed annually.

The books were elegant volumes, outside and in. The bind-

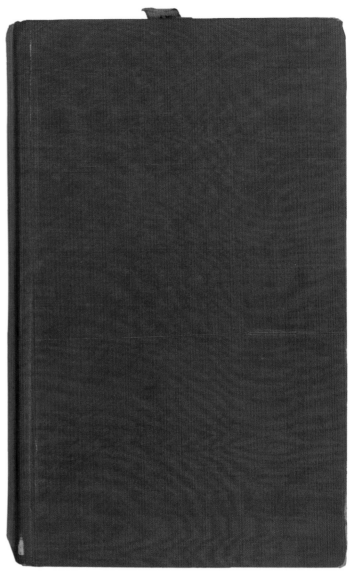

Above and opposite: The Winter's Wreath *was bound in cerise, watered-silk boards. Published in England in 1828, its main tale was by an American, John James Audubon, about a swan hunt with Cree Indians, Christmas Day, 1810.*

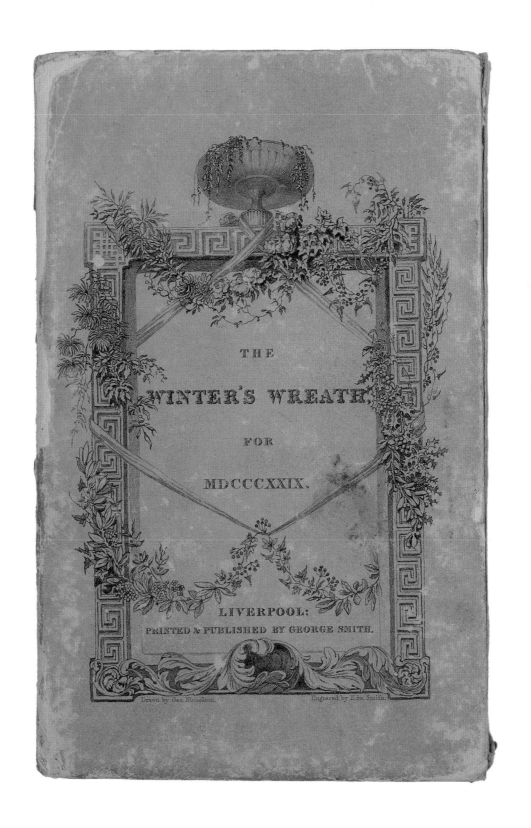

THE

WINTER'S WREATH,

FOR

MDCCCXXIX.

LIVERPOOL:
PRINTED & PUBLISHED BY GEORGE SMITH.

Drawn by Geo. Nicholson.   Engraved by Edw. Smith.

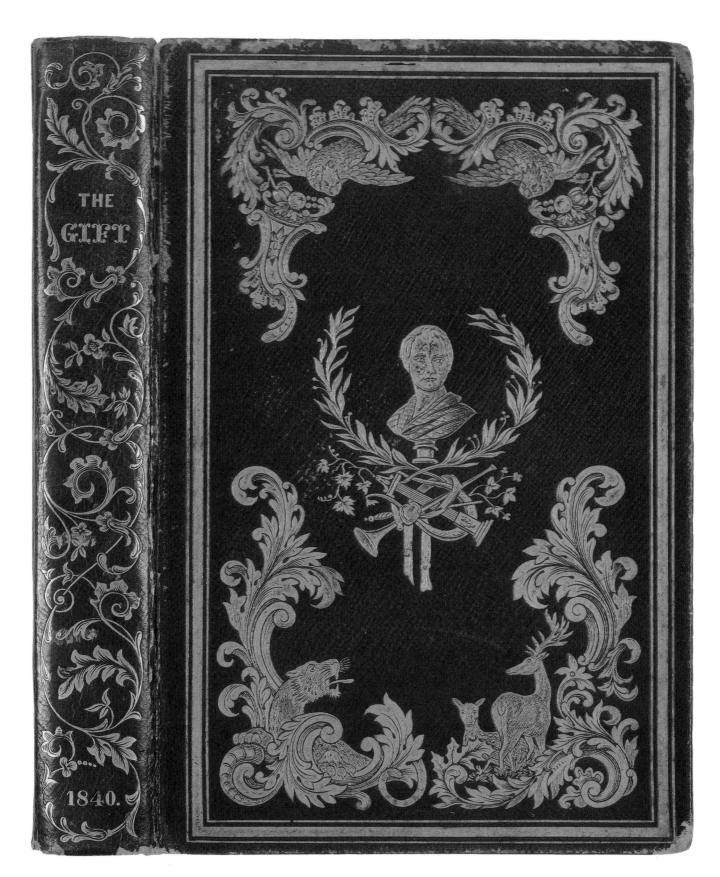

THE
GIFT

1840.

Opposite: Gift books, with their beautiful bindings, were treasured presents to be proudly displayed in the drawing-room, but not necessarily to be read! However, The Gift, 1840, contains some great reading, including Edgar Allan Poe's "William Wilson."

Below: A typical gift book had an engraved presentation page on which the giver could pen an appropriate sentiment, and displayed artwork of the highest quality. This rare, early gift book was notable for an illustration by William Blake.

ings were typically of watered-silk or embossed leather, handsome and delicious to the touch. Open a gift book and you find an engraved presentation page on which the giver could pen an appropriate sentiment to the object of his affection or esteem. There are many illustrations of the highest quality. The finest artists of the day were delighted to have their paintings reproduced, both for the liberal compensation and for the prestige: among the English, Thomas Sully, Sir Thomas Lawrence, and William Blake; in America, Thomas Doughty, Asher B. Durand, and William Sydney Mount.

The greatest care went into the engravings. An extreme example: Charles Warren spent "thirteen weeks of regular and

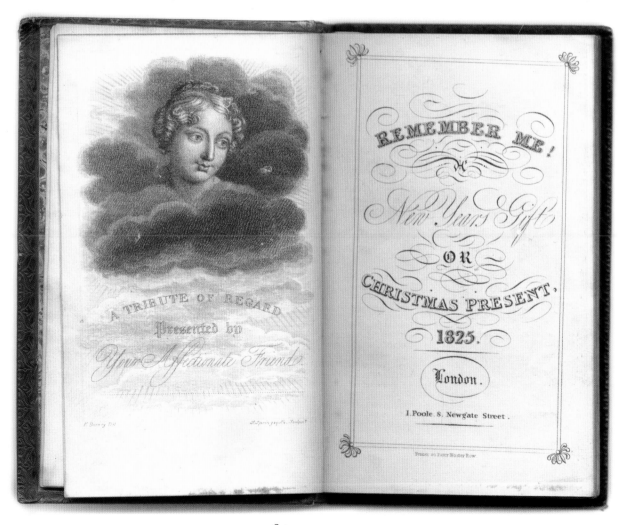

incessant exertion" on a single small plate illustrating Sir Walter Scott's "The Lady of the Lake." He was paid fifty guineas, thousands of dollars in today's money and a colossal expense for the publisher, but worth it.

Gift books were status symbols, treasures to be proudly displayed—perhaps to be leafed through but not necessarily read. As the Athenaeum commented in 1828:

The binding of The Winter's Wreath *excels that of any Annual which we have yet seen; and, considering that not the least honourable office of an Annual is to adorn the tables of drawing rooms, this is far from slight praise.*

Despite the superficial use to which these books usually were put, the best-known authors were eager to contribute to them, including Americans Henry Wadsworth Longfellow, Washington Irving, Ralph Waldo Emerson, and Harriet Beecher Stowe. Frequently, works that were to become famous appeared for the first time in gift books. For example, *The Gift* series carried the first printings of Edgar Allan Poe's masterpieces "Manuscript Found in a Bottle," "William Wilson," "The Pit and the Pendulum," and "The Purloined Letter."

The outpouring of dozens of gift books each Christmastime posed a problem. How could sufficient material be found to fill all of them? The problem was solved by borrowing from other gift books. American publishers had no compunction about purloining English material, and paying not a penny for the privilege. (Strict copyright laws were yet to come.) English publishers felt too superior to use the stuff of their less cultivated American counterparts, but they were not above some shady practices of their own. Many gift books blithely reprinted material from earlier books without attribution or reprinted a book in its entirety, only changing its cover and date. How surprised the ladies would have been had they read their "tokens of esteem."

The gift book fad faded as abruptly as it had blossomed; by

Opposite: This engraving, greatly enlarged, of the "Hiding of Moses" demonstrates William Blake's artistic genius and technical virtuosity.

Hiding of Moses

Blake del et

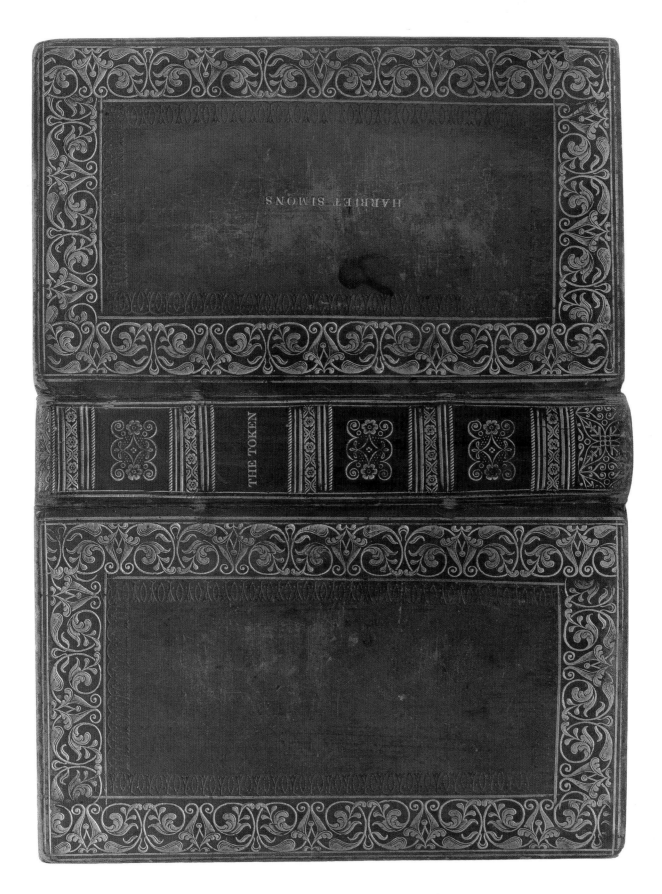

Opposite and below: Two examples of beautiful, embossed bindings: The Token, *1827, and* The Snowflake, *1840.*

the beginning of the Civil War, it was dead as a doornail, but it had an everlasting effect on our Christmas. Until the nineteenth century the giving of Christmas presents, even to children, was not commonplace. Suddenly the giving of gift books at Christmastime became the thing to do.

"A Visit from St. Nicholas" led children to expect and want presents. The gift book fad led their older sisters, mothers, and aunts to expect and want *their* presents. All these gifts had to be bought, in stores. The age of Christmas shopping, of Christmas commercialization, had begun, and the vogue of Christmas presents had been invented.

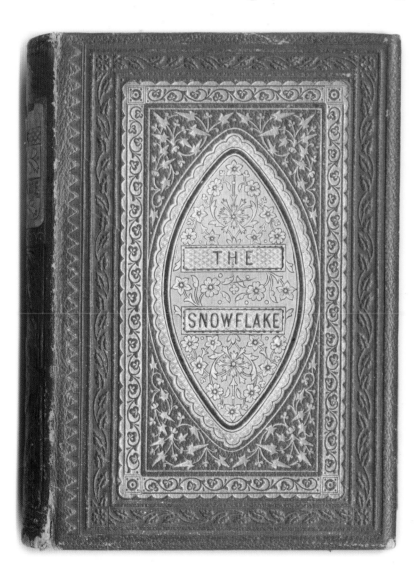

4
THE FIRST
CHRISTMAS TREES

MARTIN LUTHER AND HIS FAMILY. — FROM A PRINT PUBLISHED AT LEIPSIC.

Germany was the home of the Christmas tree. Because of those Germanic roots, many people think that the custom of Christmas trees was introduced into America, in the eighteenth century, by German immigrants to Pennsylvania and, a little later, by the Hessian troops of George III. Many people think that Prince Albert, Queen Victoria's consort, introduced the Christmas tree into England from his German homeland. In both cases, the story is not quite right.

The Christmas tree is the very emblem of Christmas today. Its roots run deep, to pagan times when evergreens were first used to decorate homes and places of worship in mid-winter. Something rather like a Christmas tree first appeared in the medieval period. The miracle, or mystery, plays of the time taught the people about religion. One of the plays, about Adam and Eve, had as a prop a fir tree hung with apples symbolizing the Garden of Eden. The tree, being ever green, symbolized immortality, and the apples represented Adam's fall.

The people of Europe were fascinated by these trees, and took to setting up their own versions in their homes. Wafers were added to the hangings, and then cookies of various shapes. These were hardly Christmas trees; they had nothing to do with the Christmas story and lacked lights, which true Christmas trees have. They were but a hint of things to come.

Still later, a curious tripod device called a "pyramid" became popular. The pyramid, a forerunner of the Christmas tree, was a wooden structure, five or so feet high. It held candles, local fruits and vegetables, and other decorations, some of which were religious in nature. The pyramids came to be used side by side with Christmas trees, and still are in some places today.

A beloved legend has come down to us about the first lighted Christmas tree.

Martin Luther was out walking one cold Christmas Eve, under a crystal-clear sky brightened by thousands of stars. The frosty trees glistened. He returned home and set up a small evergreen, which he lighted with candles to impress on his children that Christ was the Light of the World, who had lighted the sky so gloriously that Christmas Eve.

That may have been the first Christmas tree, but the event was never recorded. Wouldn't it be ironic if Luther, the famed reformer who denounced Christmas, in fact created the first Christmas tree?

The first detailed account of an actual Christmas tree reads: "At Christmas fir trees are set up in the rooms at Strasbourg and hung with roses cut from paper of many colors, apples, wafers, spangle-gold, sugar, etc. It is customary to surround it with a square frame . . . and in front . . . " The rest has been lost, so we do not know whether or not these trees were lighted with candles. It is generally accepted that Christmas trees began as a local custom in the Alsatian capital of Strasbourg, perhaps as early as the beginning of the seventeenth century.

The custom was slow to spread, possibly because it began as a Lutheran practice and was not readily accepted in Catholic areas of Germany. By the mid-eighteenth century, it had become well established in certain parts of the country. In 1758, a regulation forbade the taking of small evergreens from the forests of Salzburg (taken for Christmas trees, surely). However, surprisingly, it was not until the 1830s that Christmas trees became a national custom in Germany! They were introduced into Munich, for example, only in 1830, by the queen of Bavaria.

Opposite: First illustration of a Christmas tree in an American book. The Stranger's Gift, *1836.*

CHRISTMAS EVE.

When did the Christmas tree take root in the United States? It is highly likely that the occasional Christmas tree appeared in German settlers' homes in Pennsylvania in the eighteenth century, but it was no more a custom here than it was in Germany at the time.

And what about those Hessian troops? That leads us to another story: Christmas Eve, 1776, was bitter cold. George Washington's forces were a bedraggled, hungry, half-frozen lot. They faced the Hessian troops at Trenton, New Jersey. The Hessians had set up a small evergreen and lighted it with candles to remind them of home. They celebrated around their tree with plenty of food and grog and left their posts unguarded. Washington took advantage of the situation, and the tide of war was turned.

That is a fun story (fun for our side), but it is only a legend. There is absolutely no record of the event, no documentary evidence to support it. Indeed, the earliest written reference to Christmas trees in the United States was dated forty-five years later. On December 20, 1821, one Matthew Zahm, of Lancaster County, Pennsylvania, wrote in his diary, "Sally and our Thos. and Wm. Hensel was out for Christmas trees, on the hill at Kendrick's saw mill."

The Christmas tree finally came into its own in America through the written word. People learned about—and were entranced by—Christmas trees by reading about them rather than actually seeing them. Since the upper middle class did more reading than the rank and file, the custom began with the elite, but soon trickled down. In *The Battle for Christmas*, Stephen Nissenbaum devotes much of a forty-page chapter to this subject. I can only touch on it.

In 1835, Charles Follen, a German immigrant and Harvard professor, set up a tree for his young son Charley and two of his friends. A toy hung from every branch and there were seven dozen little wax candles. A visiting British writer named Harriet Martineau was there and recorded the scene as the drawing-room doors were thrown open:

The room seemed in a blaze, and the ornaments were so well hung on that no accident happened, except that one doll's petticoat caught fire. There was a sponge tied to the end of a stick to put out any super numerary blaze . . . The children poured in, but in a moment every voice was hushed. Their faces were upturned to the blaze, all eyes wide open, all lips parted, all steps arrested. Nobody spoke, only Charley leaped for joy . . . At last a quick pair of eyes discovered that [the tree] bore something eatable . . . and the babble began again.

Martineau wrote that she had been "present at the introduction into the new country of the German Christmas-tree," and she predicted that "the Christmas-tree will become one of the most flourishing exotics of New-England." Enchanting descriptions such as hers kindled enthusiasm for Christmas trees in the mid-1830s. It wasn't the first American Christmas tree by a long shot, but she was right in predicting a bright future.

The first illustration of a Christmas tree in an American book appeared in *The Stranger's Gift: A Christmas and New Year's Present* (1836). By the 1840s there were other pictures of Christmas trees, but one picture in particular finally created a passion for Christmas trees. That brings us back to England.

In England, as in the United States, some German immigrants probably imported their Christmas tree ritual in the early 1800s or perhaps earlier. We know that the royal family, with its German background, enjoyed its tree. Queen Charlotte, wife of George III, loved Christmas and loved her tree.

A few years after Charlotte's death, her great-niece Princess Victoria was familiar with the royal Christmas tree, as she wrote in her teenage diary on December 24, 1832:

After dinner we went upstairs . . . We went into the drawing-room near the dining room. There were two large round tables on which were placed the trees hung with lights and sugar ornaments. All the presents being placed around the tree. I had one table for myself and the Conroy family had the other together . . . I stayed up until 1/2 past 9:00.

The British people had little interest in Christmas trees, which they viewed as a Teutonic novelty. In 1840, when Victoria married Prince Albert, a German, they were not very enthusiastic about him either. But in due course, Victoria and Albert gave them a son, a new Prince of Wales, and the people got used to the family.

Then came the Big Year for the Christmas tree—1848. A full-page illustration of the royal family around their tree at Windsor Castle appeared in the *London Illustrated News*. This picture of family togetherness, tranquility, and happiness captured the imagination of the people. It was accompanied by a detailed description of the tree: about eight feet high with six tiers of branches, each with a dozen wax tapers . . . the decorations, most of which were edible, with an angel at the top . . . the arrangement of the presents, each with the recipient's name attached . . . when the tree was set up (Christmas Eve) and taken down (Twelfth Night), and so on.

Two years later, an almost identical illustration appeared in the United States, in *Godey's Lady's Book*. Victoria's coronet had been removed, along with Albert's mustache, sash, and royal insignia. Americans were captivated by what they took to be a typical "American" scene. Thus the passion for Christmas trees caught fire 150 years ago and burns unabated today.

Opposite: Queen Victoria, Prince Albert, and their children at Windsor Castle: the illustration that really launched the Christmas tree fashion. London Illustrated News, *1848.*

Below: In 1850, Godey's Lady's Book *printed the identical illustration – with some significant differences! The royal family had been transformed into the American family.*

CHRISTMAS TREE AT WINDSOR CASTLE.—DRAWN BY J. L. WILLIAMS.—(SEE NEXT PAGE.)

5
THE INVENTION
OF THE CHRISTMAS CARD

While Germany can claim credit for the first Christmas trees, the prize for the first Christmas card goes to England.

There were many forerunners of the type of card we know today. At year's end, the ancient Egyptians gave each other small, symbolic presents as tokens of good luck for the coming year; New Year messages attached to gifts have been found in Egyptian tombs of the sixth century B.C. The Romans also exchanged gifts, considered good omens, on the first day of January. For example, a pot of honey expressed the wish that the coming year would be a sweet one. "Lucky pennies" of copper with the two-faced head of Janus (indicating the past and the future) were customary New Year's gifts. Roman lamps, decorated with the winged figure of Victory, carried the inscription, "May the New Year be happy and lucky for you."

Many centuries later, the invention of printing and engraving made possible a wider dissemination of such sentiments. "Cards" and broadsides were limited to wishes for the New Year, but they often depicted Christ and so began to connect the Christmas and New Year festivals.

By the nineteenth century, "all-purpose" cards were being printed, on which the sender could fill in the name of the recipient, the occasion (birthday, Valentine, Christmas, Easter, etc.), a short greeting, and signature.

Then an energetic Englishman named Henry Cole got an idea. Later, Cole was to be involved in the founding of the Victoria & Albert Museum, the penny post, perforated postage stamps, and postcards. In 1843, he commissioned artist John Calcott Horsley to design the first Christmas card.

The card is in the form of a triptych. The center panel depicts a family party in which the adults are toasting the addressee with full glasses of wine. (This occasioned criticism from the temperance folk who worried about encouraging drunkenness.) The side panels represent the

To Mr & Lady Dorothy Nevill ... from Henry Cole . 1865

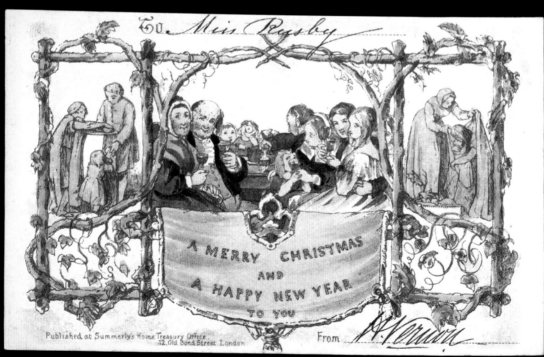

To Miss Rusby

A MERRY CHRISTMAS
AND
A HAPPY NEW YEAR
TO YOU

Published at Summerly's Home Treasury Office
12, Old Bond Street, London.

From

Opposite above: Printer's proof of the first Christmas card, given as a souvenir in 1865 by Sir Henry Cole to Mr. and Mrs. G. Wallis and family. George Wallis later became head of the Victoria and Albert Museum, of which Cole was a founder.

Opposite below: The first Christmas card, commissioned by Henry Cole and designed by John Calcott Horsley, in 1843.

Below: Typical cards of the late nineteenth century.

spirit of Christmas charity—on one the poor are being fed, and on the other given warm clothing.

At the top of the card, there is a dotted line for the name of the addressee, and at the bottom another one for the sender's signature. Also at bottom: "Published at Felix Summerly's Home Treasury Office, 12 Old Bond Street, London, by Joseph Cundall." (Felix Summerly was Henry Cole's pen name.) The card's message—"A Merry Christmas and a Happy New Year"— in my opinion, has never been improved upon.

One thousand of these cards were printed and hand-colored by a professional "hand-colorer" named Mason and sold for one shilling each, which was expensive for those days. Twenty-one of these cards are known to exist today.

For many years—until the 1950s, in fact—it was believed that the Cole/Horsley card was printed in 1846; Cole referred to that date in two memoirs written long afterward, but his memory was at fault. The matter was settled when three of the original cards, signed by the artist and dated 1843, came to light.

Here let me digress with another story. J. C. Horsley was a fine artist, a member of the Royal Academy, but he was also a bit of a prig. He objected vociferously to the new practice of British artists using models in the nude—an immoral infiltration from that degenerate Paris. His amused fellow artists dubbed him "Clothes Horsley." Whistler had fun with this comment: "Horsley soit qui mal y pense."

The first card hardly took the world by storm; the second was not designed until five years later, in 1848, by W. M. Egley. Its design is rather similar to that of the first card. In the 1850s, a few charming cards of quite different appearance were printed in England, but it wasn't until the 1860s, after the development of color printing had made the cards less expensive, that the custom of sending Christmas cards really took off.

Jonathan King was the leading authority on Christmas cards in Victorian times. In 1894, his collection of cards weighed between six and seven tons and numbered more than 163,000 varieties. And the collec-

tion was far from complete. That gives you an idea of the growth of the Christmas-card business in England in its first quarter century.

In the United States, the custom was slower to catch on. Louis Prang was "the father of the American Christmas card." Prang was a German immigrant who founded a small lithography business in Roxbury, near Boston, Massachusetts, in 1866. He perfected the lithographic process of multi-color printing. In 1874, he began printing Christmas cards in at least eight colors and sometimes as many as twenty. The cards were more expensive than the European cards but also more exquisite. They also tended to be more Christmasy, with images such as the Nativity and children playing with toys.

Today, almost two and a half billion Christmas cards are printed each year in the United States alone. Seasonal greetings are an age-old custom, and a lovely, warming one.

Above left and opposite top: The faded cover of this fringed card by Louis Prang belies the brilliant colors of the beauties within.

Left: Examples of other Prang cards.

50 Frognal   24 Dec 1895
Hampstead
        . D. W .

dear Mr Locker.

    Just a line to wish

Opposite: Kate Greenaway was one of the most popular illustrators of the late 1800s. Many of her watercolors graced Christmas cards.

Sometimes the Christmas mail just seems to be all too much. Don't you agree? Certainly Kate Greenaway did. Greenaway was one of the most popular artists of the late Victorian period. She specialized in charming, if slightly saccharine, pictures of young ladies holding bouquets of flowers and the like. An endless number of her watercolors was used to illustrate Christmas cards and almanacs. Ironically, she herself contributed to the postal clutter. Nevertheless, she wrote the following one Christmas Eve:

24 Dec. 1888
Dear [illegible]

Just a line to wish you a happy new year—though I know you dislike Christmas as much as I do—everythings put out by it our morning's letters came at past 12 this morning and now it lasts for days I really do dislike it—all the same I wish you a Happy New Year.

Yours Sincerely
Kate Greenaway

Nothing saccharine about that note! Perhaps Greenaway had second thoughts and felt it was hardly in the Christmas spirit, or that she was biting the hand that fed her. In any event, she took the trouble to decorate it with one of her watercolors.

A CHRISTMAS CAROL.

A JOVIAL Carol for Christmas time,
  Merrily, merrily sung—
Cheering the dwellings of Rich and Poor—
  Spiriting Old and Young!
Into the well of the world's deep heart
  Pouring a stream of joy,
And bidding it fresh as a fountain start,
  To bathe the jolly Old Boy.
    For as sparkling Christmas comes,
      Robed in his frost so fine;
    He chaseth tears from the hurrying years,
      And ordereth Wassail Wine!

A Christmas Carol for good Roast Beef—
  The Briton's rare old boast—
On every table in English homes—
  Plenty for guest and host!
Enough to crown the

And a tankard drunk

    For when sparkling Christmas comes,
      Sharp, with his air of cold,
    He scattereth grief—like a brave old Chief—
      And calls for his ale so old!

A Christmas Lay to a subject gay,
  Plum-pudding on the board!
Rioting free round circles of glee,
  With never a stint or hoard!
Fast and fragrant steam,
  To add to the pudding's pride;
Steeping the soul in a pleasant dream
  Of brandy sauce beside.
    For when hungry Christmas comes,
      He snorts like a fiery horse;
    And shouteth come—be quick with plum-
      Pudding and brandy sauce.

6

CHRISTMAS CAROLS, OLD AND NEW

BRIGHTON FISHERMEN CAROL SINGING.

CARROLS, FOR Christmas-day.

ALL this Night, shrill *Chauntecleere*
(*Dayes-proclaiming Trumpeter*)
Claps his wings, and lowdly Cryes,
(*Mortals, Mortals*), *wake and rise*.
See a wonder,
Heaven is under.
From the *Earth*, is risen a *Sunne*,
Shines all *Night*, though *Day* be done.

Wake (oh *Earth*), wake (*every thing*)!
Wake, and heare the *joy*, I bring.
Wake, and *joy*; for, *all* this *Night*,
Heaven, and every twinckling *Light*,
All amazing,
Still stand gazing.
Angels, Powers, and *all that bee*,
Wake ; and *joy*, this *Sunne* to see.

Haile, oh *Sunne* ! oh blessed *Light*
Sent into this *World*, by *Night* ;
Let thy *Rayes* and heavenly *Powers*,
Shine, in these darke *Soules* of *Ours*.
For most duly,
Thou art truly,
God, *and Man*, we doe confesse ;
Haile, *Oh Sunne of Righteousnesse* !

An

An other.

HArke : heare you not a *cheerefull* Noyse,
That makes *Heavens-Vault*, ring shrill with jo[y,]
See ; where (like *Starres*) bright *Angels* flye,
And thousand heavenly *Echo's* cry.
So *lowd* they chaunt, that downe to *Earth*,
Innocent *Children* heare their *Mirth*.
And sing with *them, what*, none can say,
For joy their *Prince* is *borne*, this *Day* :
Their *Prince*, their *God*, (like one of *Those*)
Is made a *Child*, and wrapt in *Clothes*.
All this is in *Times fulnesse* done :
Wee, have a *Saviour*, God, a *Sonne*.
Heaven, Earth ; *Babes, Shepheards*, Angels sing :
Oh ! *never was such Carrolling*.
Harke ; how they *all* sing at His *Birth*,
Glory to God, and *Peace on Earth*.
Vp then (my *Soule*) thy *part* desire
And sing (though but a *Base*) in this sweet *Quir[e.]*

An other.

MY *Soule*; why art thou thus deject ?
And why art thou disturbd in *Me* ?
Trust thou in God ; *his* ayde expect :
Who is the *onely helpe* for *Thee* ;
And doth thy *Sighes*, and *Sorrowes* See.

Oh ! that *Hee* once, the *Heavens* would reave,
And so come *downe*. For, *Prophets* tell,
Behold a Virgin shall conceave,
A *Sonne*, fore-nam'd *Emmanuel*,
Who shall *descend, with us* to dwell.

A

Opposite: These early carols were printed in a 1635 book of "Meditations." At the time, the Puritans were trying to put a stop to all carol singing.

The singing of carols is the oldest of our Christmas customs. It was in no way "invented" in the years 1823 to 1848, but in those same years, the ancient tradition of carols was revitalized after nearly two centuries of semidormancy. Old-time carols were collected, translated, arranged, and published, and new carols were composed.

In 1822, the year Clement Clarke Moore wrote "A Visit from St. Nicholas," a small collection was published: *Some Ancient Carols, With The Tunes to Which They Were Formerly Sung in the West of England.* The collector, Davies Gilbert, wrote wistfully in the preface:

> *"The Editor is desirous of preserving the following Carols or Christmas Songs in their actual forms, however distorted by false grammar or by obscurities, as specimens of times now passed away, and of religious feelings superseded by others of a different cast. He is anxious also to preserve them on account of the delight they afforded him in his childhood . . ."*

In 1833, a major collection of more than two hundred carols was published: *Christmas Carols, Ancient and Modern.* The collector, William Sandys, wrote a long introduction giving the history of the Christmas festival and of Christmas carols. The revival of the carol was in full swing.

What is a Christmas carol? This is not as silly a question as it may seem. Singing at festivals is as old a custom as festivals themselves. The ancient Egyptians and the Druids used music in their sacred rites, as did the Greeks and the Romans. We know from St. Paul and St. James that the earliest Christians sang psalms and hymns during their festivals and the vigils of their saints. Pliny the Younger, in a letter to Trajan in A.D. 107, wrote that the Christians "were wont to meet together on a stated day, before it was light, and sing among themselves alternately a hymn to Christ as to God."

After the Church had decreed that December 25 was to be observed as the Day of Christ's Birth, the bishops were reported to have sung hymns on Christmas Day among their clergy. But were these religious songs "carols"? Skipping ahead some 1600 years to today, we sing ditties such as "Jingle Bells" and "White Christmas." But are these "carols"?

The term "carol" originally signified songs intermingled with dancing. As time went along, it was applied to festive songs in general. And since Christmas is the most festive period in the Christian year, carols came to be thought of almost exclusively as Christmas carols.

Christmas songs have been so many and so varied that perhaps we should settle on this definition of a carol: any song that celebrates any aspect of the Christmas season.

For a thousand years, Christmas hymns were written by the clergy in the Latin of the Church of Rome and the Greek of the Eastern Orthodox Church. By the thirteenth and fourteenth centuries, Christmas songs began to appear in the languages of the people, both on the Continent and

Below: In an effort to revive the custom, carols of olden times (both words and music) were collected before they were lost forever. This was the first collection, by Davies Gilbert, 1822.

Opposite: This collection of carols, "Illustrated from Ancient Manuscripts in the British Museum," is an example of beautiful early chromolithography. 1846.

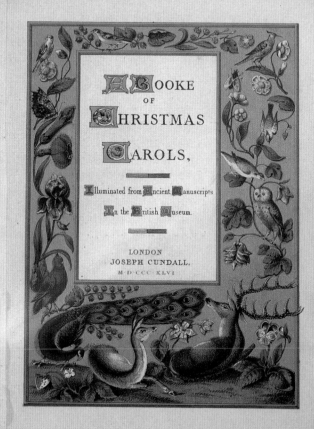

A Booke
OF
Christmas Carols,

Illuminated from Ancient Manuscripts
In the British Museum.

LONDON
JOSEPH CUNDALL,
M·D·CCC·XLVI

in England. They were still mainly written by clerics, who hoped to bring the meaning of Christmas closer to the people through this music.

During this period, the miracle and mystery plays also served to popularize religion, and carols were used in these plays. Soon the royal courts became another wellspring of carols. Many of the kings, lovers of pageantry, fostered the creation and singing of carols. Henry VIII was himself a particularly talented musician and versifier.

It is difficult to determine what the first Christmas carol was. In the case of some very early Latin hymns, we have the words only. One of the difficulties of dating early carols is the fact that the music and lyrics were often created at different times. "Good King Wenceslas" is an extreme example.

Wenceslas, incidentally, was an actual historical figure, a duke of Bohemia in the tenth century. He was a good man, a good Christian. (As opposed to his brother, who wasn't so good, and who murdered him.) The sprightly tune of "Good King Wenceslas" was composed in the thirteenth century. It wasn't until 1853, when an Englishman, John Mason Neale, discovered the tune and wrote the lyrics for it, that the carol was complete.

Another contender for the first carol is "O Come, O Come, Emmanuel." Both words and music are thought to date from the twelfth century. However, they were created separately and not assembled into a carol until 1854, by the same Mr. Neale.

The real winner may be a French carol of the thirteenth century, "The March of the Kings." This carol has the added distinction of being one of the very oldest songs of any kind to have come down to us in its original form.

The fifteenth and sixteenth centuries were the golden age of the Christmas carol. Carols were central to the celebration of the season, much more so than today. Secular carols featuring Christmas revelry and mirth were added to the religious and put to secular use. In Shakespeare's time, waits (small groups of singers and musicians) roamed the streets at night performing for small gifts of money. Many carols of the period are still popular today: "I Saw Three Ships," "Deck the Halls with Boughs of Holly," "The First Noel," and "God Rest You Merry, Gentlemen."

During the Reformation, the Puritans tried to put a stop to the singing of all but the most pious hymns as part of their efforts to stop Christmas altogether. They were not successful, but the carol custom did go into decline for two centuries, along with Christmas festivities in general. However, in the seventeenth and eighteenth centuries, a few great carols appeared, such as "Hark! The Herald Angels Sing," "O Come All Ye Faithful," "Joy to the World!" (lyrics only), and "The Twelve Days of Christmas."

In 1818, "Silent Night" was created under the most unusual circumstances. Place: St. Nicholas Church in Oberndorf, Upper Austria. Time: The day before Christmas. Problem: The organ had become rusted and wouldn't play. No music for the Christmas Eve service! Solution: The assistant priest, Father Joseph Mohr, jotted down a six-stanza poem that began, "Stille Nacht, Heilige Nacht" and took it to the local teacher, Franz Gruber, who doubled as organist. Gruber composed a simple tune. At the service, they sang it together, Gruber accompanying on the guitar. Thus was born one of the world's most popular Christmas carols.

So far, I have mentioned no carols of American origin. Surely we have contributed more than "White Christmas" and its ilk. Yes, indeed. "It Came Upon a Midnight Clear" was the first great American carol, composed in 1849. It was followed in 1857 by "We Three Kings of Orient Are" and "Jingle Bells," and in 1868 by "O Little Town of Bethlehem." This prolific twenty-year period came immediately on the heels of the years 1823 to 1848, when so many of our Christmas customs were invented.

Carol for Chriſtmas.

GOD reſt you merry, gentlemen,
　　let nothing you diſmay;
Remember Chriſt our Saviour,
　　was born on Chriſtmas day;
To ſave our ſouls from Satan's power,
　　which long had gone aſtray,
Which brings tidings of comfort and joy.

From GOD, who is our Saviour,
　　the holy angels came,
Unto ſome certain ſhepherds
　　brought tidings of the ſame,
That there was born in Bethlehem
　　the Son of GOD by name. &c.

When the ſhepherds heard theſe tidings,
　　they much rejoic'd in mind,
And left their flocks a feeding,
　　in tempeſtuous ſtorms of wind,
And ſtrait they ran to Bethlehem,
　　the Son of GOD to find. &c.

And when they came to Bethlehem,
　　where our ſweet Saviour lay,
They found him in a manger,
　　where oxen feed on hay,
And the Virgin Mary kneeling down,
　　unto the Lord did pray. &c.

GOD bleſs the ruler of this houſe,
　　and all that are within;
GOD bleſs you and your children,
　　and grant you heaven may win;
GOD bleſs you and your children,
　　that live both far and near. &c.

GOD reſt you merry, gentlemen,
　　who are within this place;
I wiſh you all, good brethren,
　　that truth you may embrace,
For the merry time of Chriſtmas,
　　is drawing on a-pace. &c.

Chriſtmas Carol.

WHen Jeſus Chriſt was twelve years old,
　　the holy Scriptures plainly told,
That he diſputed brave and bold,
　　amongſt the learned Doctors.

CHORUS.

Then praiſe the Lord both high and low,
　　for all his wond'rous works to ſhew,
That we to heaven at length may go,
　　where he in glory reigneth.

The firſt was of a pure divine,
　　by changing water into wine;
And at the marriage he did dine,
　　among the learned doctors. &c.

The next was of five loaves of bread,
　　five thouſand hungry ſouls were fed;
And ſo his glory it was ſpread,
　　thro' the whole land of Judea. &c.

Sold by M. Nayler, in Wine-Street. 1770.

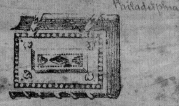

An aside which I find interesting: For centuries, "God rest you . . ." has been arguably England's most popular carol, and Dickens picked it for a role in his classic tale A Christmas Carol. *Early in the story, Scrooge is serenaded by a street urchin singing, "God rest you merry gentleman/May nothing you dismay . . ." But the old grouch, not yet imbued with the Christmas spirit,* is *dismayed, to put it mildly. The singer flees away in terror. And now, trivia buffs, you know that "God rest you . . ." is the Christmas carol of* A Christmas Carol.

Another aside, while I am writing about it: Where does the comma belong, before or after "merry"? Try it each way, and see how the meaning changes. The original, correct placement is after "merry," as shown in a 1770 broadside (opposite) although both ways are used today. Dickens sidestepped the issue by using no comma! Incidentally, note that the young singer punctiliously addresses his carol to a single gentleman.

Opposite: The custom of carols went into decline for two centuries, but did not die. This American broadside, 1770, included the most popular carol of the period, "God rest you . . ."

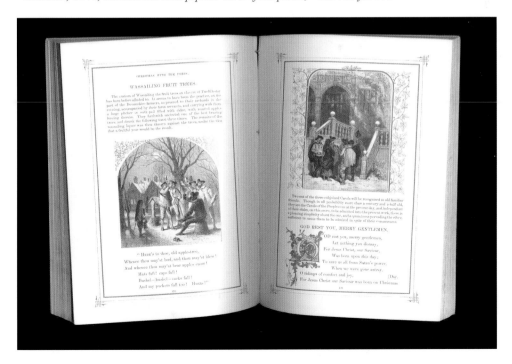

Stave I.

Marley's Ghost

Marley was dead; to begin with. There is no doubt whatever about that. The register of his burial was signed by the clergyman, the clerk, the undertaker, and the chief mourner. Scrooge signed it: and Scrooge's name was good upon 'change, for anything he chose to put his hand to. Old Marley was as dead as a door-nail.

Mind! I don't mean to say that I know, of my own knowledge, what there is particularly dead about a door-nail. I might have been inclined, myself, to regard a coffin-nail as the deadest piece of ironmongery in the trade. But the wisdom of our ancestors is in the simile; and my unhallowed hands shall not disturb it, or the Country's done for. You will therefore permit me to repeat, emphatically, that Marley was as dead as a door-nail.

Scrooge knew he was dead? Of course he did. How could it be otherwise? Scrooge and he were partners for I don't know how many years. Scrooge was his sole executor, his sole administrator, his sole assign, his sole residuary legatee, his sole friend, and sole mourner.

...th. There is no doubt whatever, about
signed by the clergyman, the clerk, the
~~chief~~ mourner. Scrooge signed it; and
for anything he chose ~~put~~ put his hand to.
it.

that I know, of my own knowledge, ~~~~~~~~ what there is
I might ~~~~~~~~ have been inclined myself
~~a~~ piece of ironmongery in the trade.
is in the simile; and my unhallowed
country's done for. You will
Marley was as dead as a door-nail.

~~~~~~~~ Of course he did. How could
partners for I don't know how many
his sole administrator, his sole
~~~~~~~~: his sole friend and sole

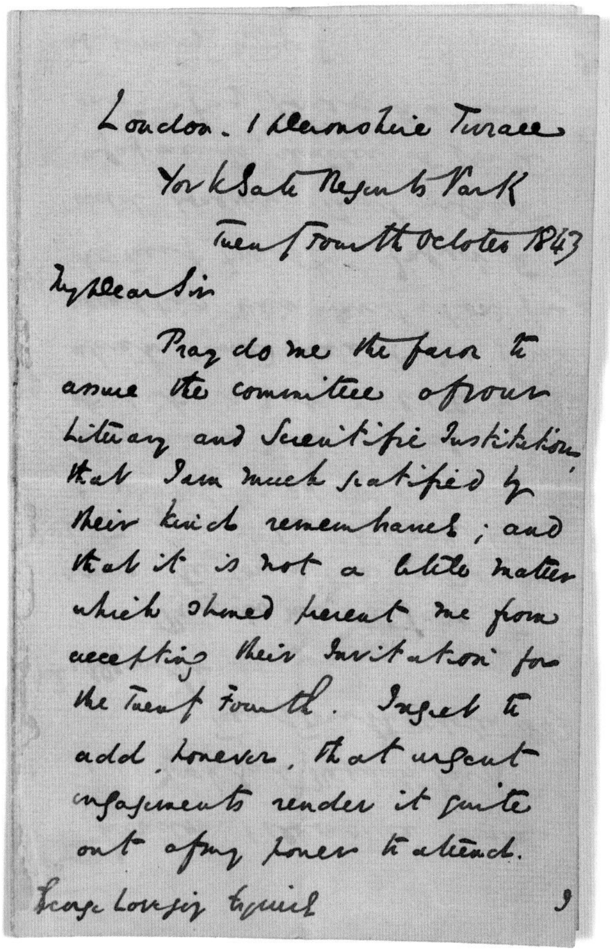

London. 1 Devonshire Terrace
York Gate Regents Park
Twenty fourth October 1843
My Dear Sir

Pray do me the favor to
assure the committee of your
Literary and Scientific Institution
that I am much gratified by
their kind remembrance; and
that it is not a little matter
which should prevent me from
accepting their Invitation for
the Twenty fourth. I regret to
add, however, that urgent
engagements render it quite
out of my power to attend.

George Lovejoy Esquire   9

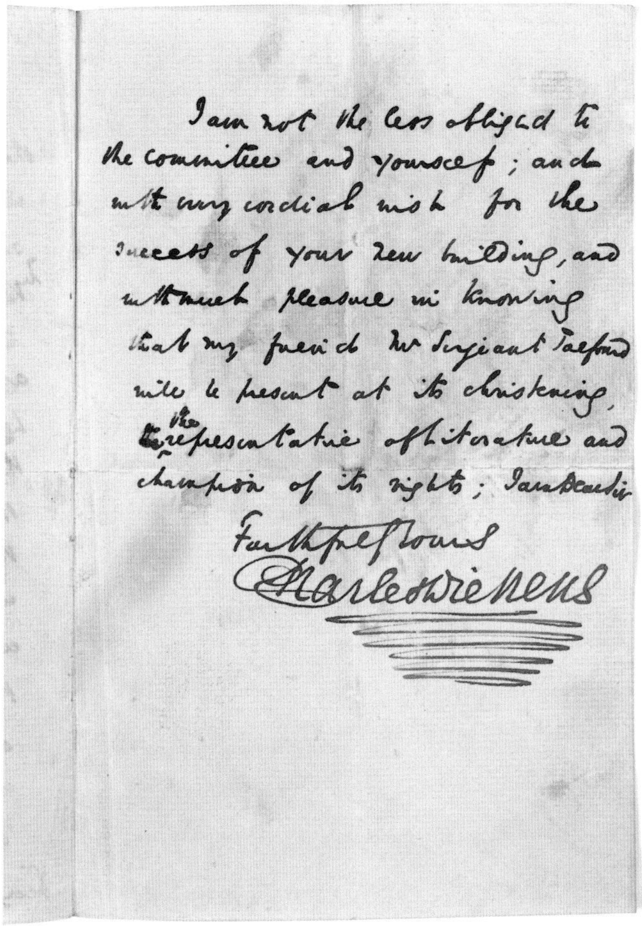

I am not the less obliged to
the committee and yourself; and
with very cordial wish for the
success of your new building, and
with much pleasure in knowing
that my friend Mr Serjeant Talfourd
will be present at its christening,
the representative of literature and
champion of its rights; I am Dear Sir

Faithfully yours
Charles Dickens

Santa Claus and Christmas presents, trees, and cards are the visible manifestations of our Christmas today, but Charles Dickens's *A Christmas Carol* personifies the *spirit* of Christmas. The story behind the creation of this masterpiece is an interesting one.

In the early part of the nineteenth century, England was suffering social problems and unrest, similar to those in the United States, brought on by the Industrial Revolution. The gap between rich and poor widened, and the well-to-do seemed indifferent to the plight of the lower classes. At Christmas, employers refused to give their workers the day off—a holiday dampener, indeed.

Writers, perhaps in the hope of reviving ancient "traditions," looked back longingly on the happy, harmonious "customs" of bygone times that had never really existed. One of these writers was Charles Dickens, but it was an American, Washington Irving, who provided the inspiration for Dickens's first writings on Christmas.

Volume II of Irving's *The Sketch Book of Geoffrey Crayon, Gent.*, published in 1819–20, began with, "There is nothing in England that exercises a more delightful spell over my imagination, than the lingerings of the holyday customs and rural games of former times." In chapters titled "Christmas," "The Stage Coach," "Christmas Eve," "Christmas Morning," and "The Christmas Dinner," the author takes us to Bracebridge Hall, where the squire royally entertains his guests with old-fashioned songs, dances, games, and sport. Every chapter was the product of Irving's romantic imagination. He invented all of it, as he had in his earlier *History of New York*, with its invented details about St. Nicholas. Irving portrayed ideal-

NOVEMBER 25, 1843.]   THE BRITANNIA.

ized Christmases that did not exist at the time and never had. Dickens enjoyed—we might even say, borrowed from—Irving's accounts of these supposed Christmas customs.

Dickens first wrote about Christmas in *Sketches by Boz* (1836). The last chapter in Volume I is "A Christmas Dinner" (modeled on Irving's chapter of the same title). It is clearly a harbinger of the Cratchits' Christmas dinner in *A Christmas Carol*—not only in its warm feeling of family togetherness and jollity but in its hint of a tiny figure yet to come:

> *Look on the merry faces of your children as they sit round the fire. One little seat may be empty—one slight form that gladdened the father's heart, and roused the mother's pride to look upon, may not be there. Dwell not upon the past— think not that one short year ago, the fair child now resolving into dust sat before you, with the bloom of health upon its cheek, and the gay unconsciousness of infancy in its joyous eye.*

Sketches by Boz was followed by *The Posthumous Papers of the Pickwick Club* (1837). Dickens's description of the festivities of the Pickwickian Dingley Dell, from stagecoach to Christmas dinner, owed much to Irving's account of the doings at Bracebridge Hall. After publication of *The Pickwick Papers*, it would be another six years before Dickens wrote again on Christmas. This time, the inspiration would be his and his alone.

The first nine months of 1843 were worrying ones for Dickens. The first monthly installments of *Martin Chuzzlewit* were poorly received, and his reputation was beginning to suffer. His *American Notes* (1842), highly critical of our democratic practices, had understandably irritated Americans and sales were off in the United States. (Equally understandably, the British loved it.) His publishers, Chapman and Hall, wanted to reduce his drawing account from £200 to £150, and Dickens was living beyond his means in a large house on Devonshire Terrace, with a wife pregnant with their fifth child.

Adding to his disturbed state of mind was a growing sense of social conscience; he had become increasingly preoccupied with the plight of the poor, the "child labor question," and the fact that no one was doing anything about these appalling problems. Parish orphans and children of the destitute were routinely put to work at the age of seven, some as young as three! Ill-fed and ill-clothed, they labored fifteen to eighteen hours a day in the coal mines. What little they earned went directly to the orphanages or into their parents' pockets. Dickens not only read reports on the shocking conditions but went out of his way to witness the conditions for himself. He visited the mines in Cornwall and the wretched institutions for the poor in the grubbiest parts of London.

Anguished and incensed, he considered writing a pamphlet, to be called "An Appeal to the People of England, on Behalf of the Poor Man's Child." Before he could do it, he accepted an invitation to speak on October 5, 1843 at the Atheneum, a charitable institution for the working class in Manchester. He spoke passionately on the need for greater education of the poor in order to combat ignorance and want.

The enthusiastic applause persuaded him that good people could be enlisted in the battle to improve the lot of the poor, and that he should throw himself "upon the truthful feeling of the people." While broodingly walking the streets of Manchester, a better idea than a pamphlet occurred to him—an idea for a story.

Dickens hurried back to London, where he began feverishly writing, while at the same time turning out what he referred to as his "Chuzzlewit agonies." He worked night and day; everything else had to be set aside. A letter dated "Twenty Fourth October 1843" from Dickens to a George Lovejoy reads:

> *Pray do me the favor to assure the Committee of our Literary and Scientific Institution that I am much satisfied by their kind remembrances; and that it is not a little*

Opposite: Mr. and Mrs. Fezziwig at the Ball, by John Leech. This is the rare "experimental" issue of the Carol, *with the title page printed in red and green instead of the final red and blue.*

Below: The first ten copies of the Carol *were delivered to Dickens on December 17, 1843, only ten weeks after its conception!*

Mr Fezziwig's Ball.

A CHRISTMAS CAROL.

IN PROSE.

BEING

A Ghost Story of Christmas.

BY

CHARLES DICKENS.

WITH ILLUSTRATIONS BY JOHN LEECH.

LONDON:
CHAPMAN & HALL, 186, STRAND.

MDCCCXLIV.

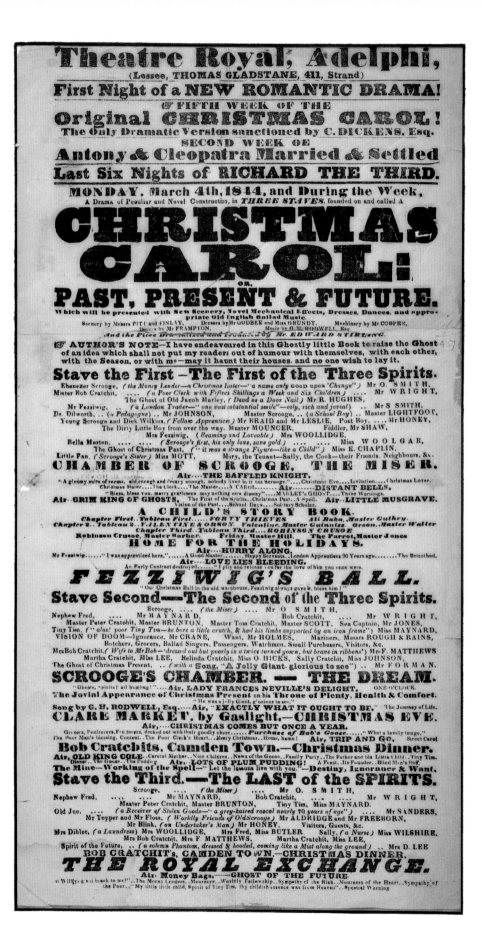

Opposite: Within two months, dramatizations of the Carol *appeared on the London stages. All were pirated versions; Dickens made not a penny from them.*

matter which should prevent me from accepting their invitation for the Twenty Fourth. I regret to add, however, that urgent engagements render it quite out of my power to attend.

The "not a little matter" and "urgent engagements" were most likely the writing of the *Carol*. A subsequent letter from Dickens, this one to Macvey Napier and by coincidence also dated October 24, tells of the necessity to postpone all projects other than his present one:

I plunged headlong into a little scheme ... set an artist to work upon it; and put it wholly out of my own power to touch the Edinburgh subject until after Christmas is turned. For carrying out the notion I speak of, and being punctual with Chuzzlewit, will occupy every moment of my working time up to the Christmas Holidays.

By October 24, Dickens had been working on his "little scheme" for less than three weeks but had already written enough to hire illustrator John Leech. Less than a month later the manuscript was complete. (This original manuscript now belongs to the Morgan Library, where it is on view each Christmastime.)

Dickens became so possessed by his story that, as he described, he "wept and laughed and wept again, and excited himself in a most extraordinary manner in the composition; and thinking whereof he walked about the black streets of London, fifteen and twenty miles many a night when all sober folks had gone to bed."

On November 25, a tiny newspaper advertisement, less than one inch deep, announced the forthcoming publication of *A Christmas Carol*, and on December 17, only ten weeks after its conception, and two days before publication date, the first ten copies were delivered to Dickens. He immediately inscribed, and dated, all ten copies for friends.

Considering the speed with which the *Carol* was written, one might think that Dickens wrote it effortlessly, that the words simply flowed from his pen. Nothing could be further from the truth. In his manuscript, virtually every sentence has been rewritten, with the exception of the first, "Marley was dead: to begin with." As new editions came along, the perfectionist continued to make changes.

For this book, Dickens requested an unusual arrangement with his publishers, Chapman and Hall: He would pay all publishing expenses and pocket all profits, with the publishers getting only a fixed commission on the number of books sold. This deal would prove to be unfortunate for Dickens.

Dickens wanted to produce a little gem of a book that would be perfect in every respect and yet priced modestly (five shillings a copy) for wide consumption. Not only would it be illustrated, but four of the illustrations would be in color. (In a first edition of 6,000, this meant the immediate hand-coloring of 24,000 engravings.) He experimented endlessly with the format of the book, first printing the title page in red and green with green endpapers (nice Christmas colors), but the green type was too drab and the endpapers tended to smudge and rub off. He then switched to a red and blue title page with yellow endpapers. He even tried pink endpapers, but that was a nonstarter. And all such experimentation cost money.

The book was an instantaneous success. The entire first edition was sold out by Christmas, many copies on Christmas Day itself, which was not yet a national holiday. Early demand was so great that almost immediately the printers had to use whatever supplies were on hand, including the "experimental" green endpapers and even some of the red-and-green title pages, until all were exhausted. The result was that many, perhaps most, of the volumes of the first edition were "mixed" copies.

Dickens lost money on the first edition. He had expected to clear £1,000 on the first printing, but he had spent too much on production and charged too little for the book, and the profits dwindled to £230. But worse was to come.

On January 6, 1844, Parley's Illuminated Library pirated the

Right: Facsimile of the author's "Prompt Copy," showing how Dickens cut the Carol *for his public readings.*

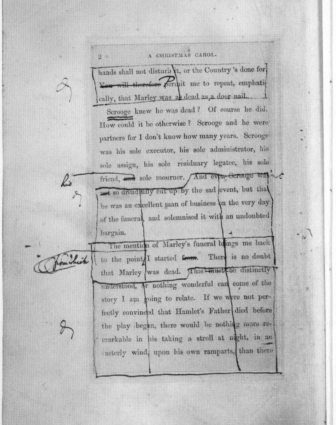

hands shall not disturb it, or the Country 's done for. You will therefore permit me to repeat, emphatically, that Marley was as dead as a door-nail.

Scrooge knew he was dead? Of course he did. How could it be otherwise? Scrooge and he were partners for I don't know how many years. Scrooge was his sole executor, his sole administrator, his sole assign, his sole residuary legatee, his sole friend, and sole mourner. And even Scrooge was not so dreadfully cut up by the sad event, but that he was an excellent man of business on the very day of the funeral, and solemnised it with an undoubted bargain.

The mention of Marley's funeral brings me back to the point I started from. There is no doubt that Marley was dead. This must be distinctly understood, or nothing wonderful can come of the story I am going to relate. If we were not perfectly convinced that Hamlet's Father died before the play began, there would be nothing more remarkable in his taking a stroll at night, in an easterly wind, upon his own ramparts, than there

would be in any other middle-aged gentleman rashly turning out after dark in a breezy spot—say Saint Paul's Churchyard for instance—literally to astonish his son's weak mind.

Scrooge never painted out Old Marley's name. There it stood, years afterwards, above the warehouse door: Scrooge and Marley. The firm was known as Scrooge and Marley. Sometimes people new to the business called Scrooge Scrooge, and sometimes Marley, but he answered to both names. It was all the same to him.

Oh! But he was a tight-fisted hand at the grindstone, Scrooge! a squeezing, wrenching, grasping, scraping, clutching, covetous old sinner! Hard and sharp as flint, from which no steel had ever struck out generous fire; secret, and self-contained, and solitary as an oyster. The cold within him froze his old features, nipped his pointed nose, shrivelled his cheek, stiffened his gait; made his eyes red, his thin lips blue; and spoke out shrewdly in his grating voice. A frosty rime was on his head, and on his eyebrows, and his wiry chin. He

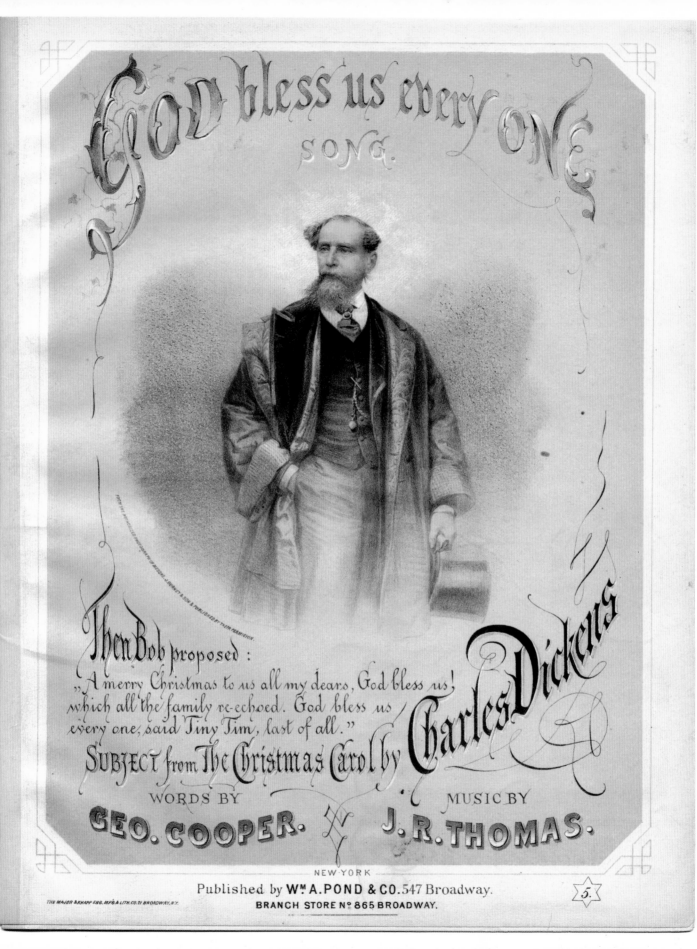

The Carol was so popular that it spawned many off-shoots, such as this sheet music and parlor game.

Carol, publishing *A Christmas Ghost Story reoriginated from the original by Charles Dickens, Esq. and analytically condensed for this work.* Dickens sued and won, but Parley's went bankrupt. Dickens was stuck with legal expenses of £700. So Charles Dickens actually lost almost £500 on the first edition of his masterpiece.

That was only the beginning of piracy. The *Carol* was immediately printed internationally, usually without Dickens's sanction. In 1844, the Philadelphia publishing house of Carey & Hart came out with a very good copy. This volume was set from the London first printing and illustrated with redrawn plates of Leech's artwork. For some reason, the Americans used Leech's "Marley's Ghost" as the frontispiece (instead of the Fezziwigs). The redrawings were good, but they lacked Leech's touch. Also in 1844, the New York publishers Harper & Brothers published an inexpensive edition of the *Carol* without illustrations. Dickens made not a penny from either printing.

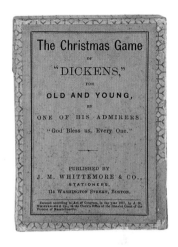

The one exception to the piracy of the book took place in Germany. Earlier in 1843, Bernhard Tauchnitz of Leipzig had secured the rights to authorized editions of the works of English authors, Dickens included. Advance proofs were provided to Tauchnitz's company, and he advertised that his "edition sanctioned by the author" would be published simultaneously with the London edition. Ironically, the earliest printing of the *Carol* may not have been in England but in Germany a day or two earlier.

Piracy was not limited to the book itself, but extended to dramatizations of the *Carol*. The first performance of the *Original*

Christmas Carol took place in London little more than one month after the publication of the book and was quickly followed by other pirated productions.

Despite the initial financial disappointments of the *Carol*, Dickens knew he was on to a good thing. He followed up with four more Christmas books: *The Chimes* (1844), *The Cricket on the Hearth* (1845), *The Battle of Life* (1846), and *The Haunted Man* (1848). All of these sold even better than the *Carol*. While Dickens knew he was riding a winner with his Christmas books, so did every other writer and publisher. Numerous people began writing books for the holidays. William Makepeace Thackeray got the snowball rolling with his six Christmas books (1847–55), going Dickens one better.

In 1847, Hans Christian Andersen published *A Christmas Greeting to My English Friends*, a volume of seven fairy tales dedicated to Dickens. A snowstorm of holiday books by writers of lesser talent began, such as *The Inundation* (1848) by Mrs. Gore. These books were as popular in the United States as in England. Charles Dickens had invented a new genre: holiday books.

Holiday books differed from gift books (which they soon supplanted) in content and purpose. Holiday books were written for Christmas, published for the reading public, and modestly priced. Gift books were elaborately produced compilations, written without Christmas in mind, and were designed to be given as presents, with fine engravings, and priced accordingly.

In the mid-1850s, Dickens undertook public readings of some of his works—to make money but also to satisfy his love of being on stage (frankly, he was a bit of a ham). The *Carol* was a favorite, with

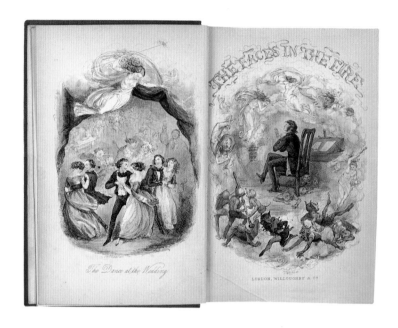

Opposite: Dickens's five Christmas books gave birth to a new genre: "holiday books." Thackeray wrote six of them. This one, illustrated by the author, was his last and most successful. 1855.

Above: A slavish copy of the Dickens volumes: same size, same red cloth cover, yellow endpapers, gilt edges, same format in virtually all respects. But not the same writing! 1850.

POOR BULBO IS ORDERED FOR EXECUTION.

[Frontispiece.

THE

ROSE AND THE RING;

OR, THE

HISTORY OF PRINCE GIGLIO AND PRINCE BULBO.

A Fire-Side Pantomime for Great and Small Children.

BY MR. M. A. TITMARSH,

Author of "The Kickleburys on the Rhine," "Mrs. Perkins's Ball," &c. &c.

W. M. Thackeray

LONDON:
SMITH, ELDER, AND CO., 65, CORNHILL.
1855.

The Dream.

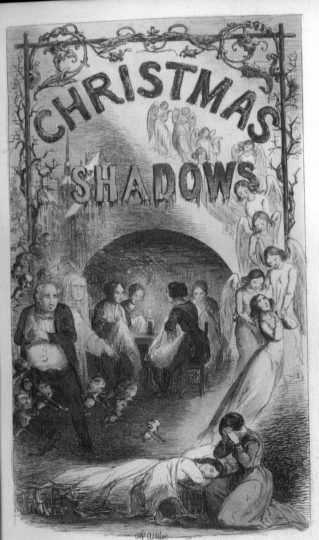

LONDON: T. C. NEWBY, 30, WELBECK STREET, CAVENDISH SQUARE.

the audience and with Dickens himself. In the interest of time, he had to cut out more than half the story, but did it so skillfully that the audience never realized they had not heard all of their beloved *Carol*. In his reader copy, Dickens was still editing, seeking the perfect word or turn of phrase.

It would be hard to overestimate the influence *A Christmas Carol* had on our Christmas. For the past 158 years, it has remained the most popular Christmas story. When Dickens created Ebenezer Scrooge, he invented a character almost as familiar as Santa Claus himself. John Leech's frontispiece of Mr. and Mrs. Fezziwig at the ball is a beloved Christmas picture, reproduced year after year on tens of thousands of Christmas cards. Other fine illustrators such as Arthur Rackham, Everett Shinn, and Ronald Searle have added to the delight of the *Carol*. Dramatizations of the *Carol* were smash hits in London in 1844. They are still hits on Broadway, on television, and in the movies.

The influence of the Carol transcends all such specifics. Thackeray wrote of it:

> *I believe it occasioned immense hospitality throughout England; was the means of lighting up hundreds of kind fires at Christmas time; caused a wonderful outpouring of Christmas good-feeling; of Christmas punch-brewing; an awful slaughter of Christmas turkeys, and roasting and basting of Christmas beef.*

This was as true in the United States as in England. Dickens was horrified by the indifference of the comfortable classes to the awful plight of the poor. He believed that a change of heart among the "good people" was the only solution to ignorance and want. The miserly Scrooge was the embodiment of callous indifference. The story of his conversion is the story of the reawakening of a human spirit, of the Christmas spirit. By writing *A Christmas Carol*, and by his public readings of the tale, Dickens did more than any other man to restore the Christmas spirit and to revive the Christmas festival in England and America.

The curtains of his bed were drawn aside.

Above: A long procession of illustrators followed in the steps of John Leech. C. E. Brock was one of the most prolific, and charming, illustrators at the turn of the century. 1905.

Opposite: The exhilarating picture of Mr. and Mrs. Fezziwig by Everett Shinn personifies, for the author of this book, the spirit of Christmas.

Above: S. Eytinge, Jr. drew the Spirit of Christmas Present, Scrooge, and the two wretched figures of Ignorance and Want. 1868.

Opposite: The Spirit of Christmas Yet to Come leads Scrooge to his own (possible) grave. Everett Shinn, 1938.

Human beings like to have a good time. Despite the hardships of life, or rather because of them, mankind has always found reason to celebrate. Regular celebrations punctuate the year, temporarily relieving men and women of their worries and of the tedium of their daily lives.

In ancient pagan times, the greatest of the year's celebrations took place at the time of the winter solstice. These midwinter festivals celebrated the gods of harvest, the return of the sun, and the beginning of a new year. In their way, the pagans celebrated eternal life.

In the Christian world, Christmas is our great midwinter festival. We celebrate the birth of Jesus. In our own way, we celebrate eternal life as taught by Jesus. The life of the soul.

Our secular festivities have an age-old pagan ring to them, such as feasting, drinking, and the decoration of our houses with evergreens and lights. It is easy to think of our Christmas customs and traditions as being age-old, but they are not. Up to the nineteenth century, Christmas as we know it had never existed in this country. No Santa Claus, no shopping for presents, no Christmas trees, no Christmas cards, no Scrooge. Between 1823 and 1848—a surprisingly short twenty-five-year period—all these "traditions" were invented.

Hooray for the inventions, say I. They give us all a good time.

Books marked with an asterisk (*) provided most of the source material for this book.

Ashton, John. *A righte Merrie Christmasse!!! The Story of Christ-tide.* London: Leadenhall Press, (n.d.)

Beaton, Katherine. *The Real Santa Claus.* London: H & B Publications, 1986.

* Buday, George. *The History of the Christmas Card.* London: Rockliff, 1954.

Bullen, A. H. *Carols and Poems from the Fifteenth Century to the Present Time.* London: John C. Nimmo, 1880.

Calhoun, Philo and Heaney, Howell J. Dickens' *"Christmas Carol"* After A Hundred Years: *A Study In Bibliographical Evidence.* *The Papers of the Bibliographical Society of America*: Volume Thirty-nine, Fourth Quarter, 1945.

Campbell, R. J. *The Story of Christmas.* New York: Macmillan, 1941.

Chalmers, Irene. *The Great American Christmas Almanac.* New York and Ontario: Penguin Books, 1988.

Chase, Ernest Dudley. *The Romance of Greeting Cards.* Boston: The University Press, 1926.

Coffin, Tristram Potter. *The Book of Christmas Folklore.* New York: The Seabury Press, 1973.

Count, Earl W. *4000 Years of Christmas.* New York: Henry Schuman, 1948.

Crippen, T. G. *Christmas and Christmas Lore.* London and Glasgow: Blackie & Son, 1927.

Dawson, W. F. *Christmas: Its Origin and Associations.* London: Elliot Stock, 1902.

Del Re, Gerard and Patricia. *The Christmas Almanack.* Garden City New York: Doubleday, 1979.

Dolby, George. *Charles Dickens As I Knew Him.* London: Everett, 1885.

Ebon, Martin. *Saint Nicholas: Life and Legend.* New York: Harper & Row, 1975.

Faxon, Frederick W. *Literary Annuals and Gift Books.* Reprinted from original edition of 1912. Pinner, Middlesex: Private Libraries Association, 1973.

* Foley, Daniel J. *The Christmas Tree.* Philadelphia and New York: Chilton, 1960.

* Hadfield, Miles and John. *The Twelve Days of Christmas.* London: Cassell, 1961.

* Hearn, Michael Patrick. *The Annotated Christmas Carol.* New York: Clarkson N. Potter, 1976.

Hervey, Thomas K. *The Book of Christmas.* London: William Spooner, 1836.

Hottes, Alfred Carl. *1001 Christmas Facts and Fancies.* New York: T. De La Mare, 1957.

H. V. (Editor). *Christmas with the Poets: A Collection of Songs, Carols, and Descriptive Verses.* London: Bell & Daldy, 1851.

* Jones, Charles W. *Saint Nicholas of Myra, Bari, and Manhattan Biography of a Legend.* Chicago and London: University of Chicago Press, 1978.

Mabie, Hamilton, W. *The Book of Christmas*: New York: MacMillan, 1924.

Matthews, John. *The Winter Solstice.* Wheaton, Ill. and Madras, India: Quest Books, 1998.

Miall, Antony and Peter. *The Victorian Christmas Book.* New York: Pantheon, 1978.

Miles, Clement A. *Christmas in Ritual and Tradition Christian and Pagan.* London and Leipsic: T. Fisher Unwin, 1912.

* Nissenbaum, Stephen. *The Battle for Christmas.* New York: Alfred A. Knopf, 1996.

Osborne, E. Allen. *The Facts About "A Christmas Carol."* London: The Bradley Press, 1937.

Rickert, Edith. *Ancient English Christmas Carols 1400-1700.* New York: Chatto & Windus, 1910.

* Sandys, William. *Christmas Carols, Ancient and Modern.* London: Richard Beckley, 1833.

* Sandys, William. *Christmastide its History, Festivities, and Carols.* London: John Russell Smith, (1852).

* Sansom, William. *A Book of Christmas*, New York: McGraw-Hill, 1968.

* Studwell, William E. *The Christmas Carol Reader.* New York and London: Harrington Park Press, 1995.

* Thompson, Ralph. *American Literary Annuals & Gift Books.* New York: H. W. Wilson, 1936.

Tille, Alexander. *Yule and Christmas.* London: David Nutt, 1899.

Voorsanger, Catherine. *Art and the Empire City New York, 1825-1861.* Hoover and John K. Howat. Metropolitan Museum of Art, New York. New Haven and London: Yale University Press 2000.

Warren, Nathan B. *The Holidays: Christmas, Easter, and Whitsuntide.* New York: Hurd and Houghton, 1868.

White, Gleeson. *Christmas Cards and Their Chief Designers.* London: The Studio, 1895.

I am grateful to my fellow members of the Grolier Club for inviting me to exhibit part of my collection at the Club in December, 2000. And I thank Roberta Smith and Dinitia Smith of the New York Times for writing so generously about the exhibition. This led Paul Gottlieb, then-president of Harry Abrams, and Karyn Gerhard, my editor-to-be, to visit the exhibition and to ask me to write this book. From the start, their enthusiastic support has been most encouraging to this neophyte book-writer. I am indebted to Beth Middleworth, who designed the book with flair and imagination. I salute my assistant Alice Sosa, who typed and re-typed the whole thing. Alice is the only person on Earth who can read my wretched, minuscule handwriting. Including me.

Finally, I thank my wife Elly for cheerfully enduring my benign neglect. And for her patience. "Honey, how does this sound?" preceded reading her my every last prose gem. Oh, I almost forgot to thank my friends and dinner partners over the past year. Talk about patience! Not one of them ever exploded with, "Can't you ever talk about anything but that damned book?!"

Editor: Karyn Gerhard
Designer: Beth Middleworth
Production Director: Hope Koturo

Photography: Bob Lorenzson: 14, 26 right, 27, 37, 34, 37, 38, 42–43,
45, 81, 97, 100, 109, 110, 113, 117, 120; B. Middleworth: 6 all, 7 all,
10, 12, 18, 21, 25, 39, 43, 58–9, 60, 61, 65, 69, 70–71, 72, 76–7, 82–3,
86, 87, 88 bottom, 89 bottom, 90, 91, 92–93, 96, 101, 102–3, 108,
114, 118; Zindman/Fremont: 2, 8, 9, 13, 16–17, 20, 21, 22, 24, 26 left,
28, 30–31, 32, 35, 36, 40–41, 44, 46, 48, 49, 51, 52, 53, 54 all, 55 all,
56 all, 57 all, 62, 63, 64, 67, 68, 75, 78–9, 84, 88 top, 89 top, 94, 98,
99, 104, 106, 115, 116, 119, 121, 122, 123, 125.

Library of Congress Cataloging-in-Publication Data

Elliott, Jock.
  Inventing Christmas : how our holiday came to be / Jock Elliott.
    p. cm.
Includes bibliographical references.
  ISBN 0-8109-3493-0 (hardcover)
1. Christmas—History. I. Title.
  GT4985 .E413 2002
  394.2663—dc21

                          2002003210

Published in 2002 by Harry N. Abrams, Incorporated, New York
All rights reserved. No part of the contents of this book may be
reproduced without the written permission of the publisher.

Printed and bound in Hong Kong
10 9 8 7 6 5 4 3 2 1

Harry N. Abrams, Inc.
100 Fifth Avenue
New York, N.Y. 10011
www.abramsbooks.com

Abrams is a subsidiary of

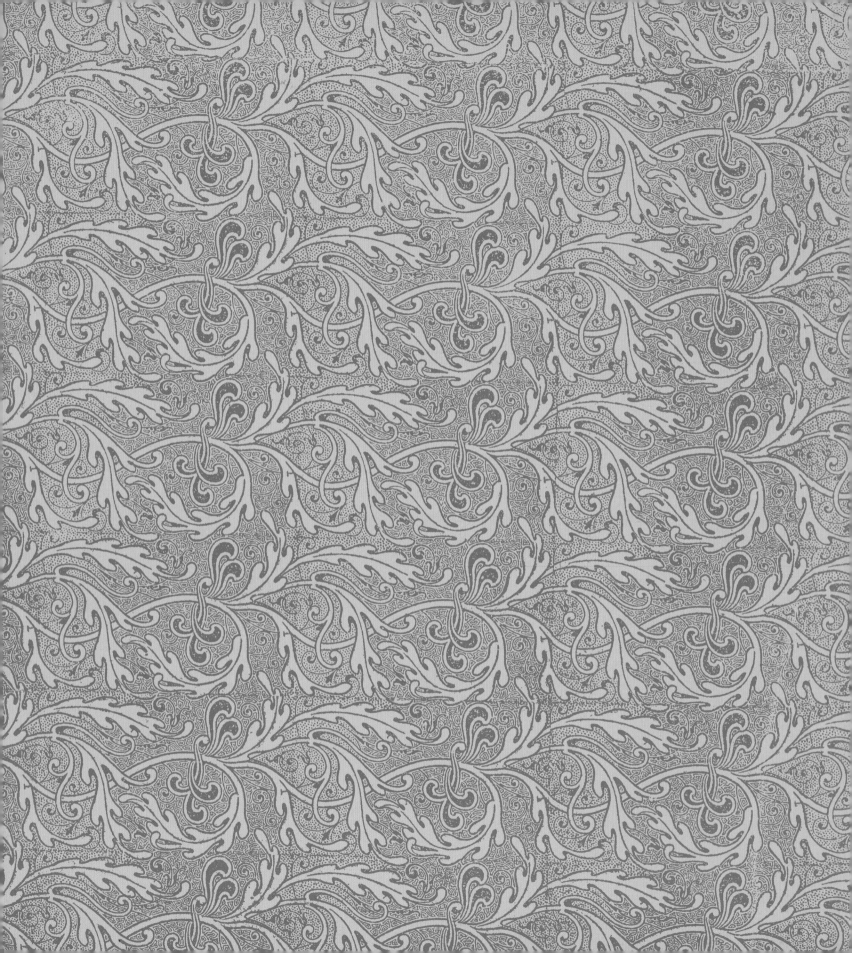